"When Ray Ortlund speaks, I listen. My generation has grown in knowledge but needs sages. Pastor Ray is that to us. Pick up this resource and hear from a man who espouses theological depth matched by gospel grace."

Eric M. Mason, Lead Pastor, Epiphany Fellowship, Philadelphia, Pennsylvania; President, Thriving; author, *Manhood Restored*

"Churches don't make the gospel true, but when 'the sweetness of the Lord' is upon us, the church becomes a powerful testimony of God's grace. With both realism and hope, Ray Ortlund tells us how that grace can thrive among us— even as broken as we are—so that Christ's glory will radiate from us."

Bryan Chapell, President Emeritus, Covenant Theological Seminary; Senior Pastor, Grace Presbyterian Church, Peoria, Illinois

"Ray Ortlund weaves together profound biblical reflection on how gospel doctrine must lead to gospel culture with choice quotations from great saints in church history. A must read for any church that wants to help rather than hinder the lost in being attracted to Christ."

Craig L. Blomberg, Distinguished Professor of New Testament, Denver Seminary

"Compelling. Convicting. Encouraging. Probing. And most of all, entrancing. What a beautiful vision of what the church can be through the power of the gospel. How evident it is that the gospel has penetrated Ortlund's own heart. Read it. Pray through it. Ask God to use its message mightily in your church and in many other churches as well."

Thomas R. Schreiner, James Buchanan Harrison Professor of New Testament Interpretation, The Southern Baptist Theological Seminary

"Pastor-scholar Ray Ortlund, in his newest book, brings out the goodness in the good news. And a church that doesn't show this goodness in their life together, says he, undermines the very gospel they preach. It's a good argument, and worthwhile."

Mark Dever, Senior Pastor, Capitol Hill Baptist Church, Washington, DC; President, 9Marks

"In this incisive book, Ray Ortlund does the necessary and compelling work of connecting the life-giving gospel to the lived experience and witness of the church. His vision for gospel cultures that bloom in the rich soil of gospel doctrine will capture those who desire to see the world captivated by Christ."

Stephen T. Um, Senior Minister, Citylife Presbyterian Church, Boston, Massachusetts; co-author, *Why Cities Matter*

THE GOSPEL

9Marks: Building Healthy Churches

Edited by Mark Dever and Jonathan Leeman

Expositional Preaching: How We Speak God's Word Today,
Ⅰ David Helm

Sound Doctrine: How a Church Grows in the Love and Holiness
Ⅰ *of God,* Bobby Jamieson

The Gospel: How the Church Portrays the Beauty of Christ,
Ⅰ Ray Ortlund

Evangelism: How the Whole Church Speaks of Jesus,
Ⅰ J. Mack Stiles

Church Membership: How the World Knows Who Represents
Ⅰ *Jesus,* Jonathan Leeman

Church Discipline: How the Church Protects the Name of Jesus,
Ⅰ Jonathan Leeman

Church Elders: How to Shepherd God's People Like Jesus,
Ⅰ Jeramie Rinne

BUILDING HEALTHY CHURCHES

THE GOSPEL

HOW THE
CHURCH
PORTRAYS THE
BEAUTY OF
CHRIST

RAY ORTLUND

WHEATON, ILLINOIS

Cover design: Dual Identity inc.
Cover image(s): Wayne Brezinka for brezinkadesign.com

First printing 2014

Printed in the United States of America

Trade paperback ISBN: 978-1-4335-4083-7
ePub ISBN: 978-1-4335-4086-8
PDF ISBN: 978-1-4335-4084-4
Mobipocket ISBN: 978-1-4335-4085-1

Library of Congress Cataloging-in-Publication Data

Ortlund, Raymond C.
   The gospel : how the church portrays the beauty of
Christ / Ray Ortlund.
      pages cm. — (9marks: building healthy churches)
   Includes bibliographical references and index.
   ISBN 978-1-4335-4083-7 (hc)
   1. Jesus Christ--Person and offices. I. Title.
BV203.O78   2014
262—dc23   2013033035

To Immanuel Church,
where gospel doctrine and
gospel culture converge,
for God's glory alone

CONTENTS

SERIES PREFACE

Do you believe it's your responsibility to help build a healthy church? If you are a Christian, we believe that it is.

Jesus commands you to make disciples (Matt. 28:18–20). Jude says to build yourselves up in the faith (Jude 20–21). Peter calls you to use your gifts to serve others (1 Pet. 4:10). Paul tells you to speak the truth in love so that your church will become mature (Eph. 4:13, 15). Do you see where we are getting this?

Whether you are a church member or leader, the Building Healthy Churches series of books aims to help you fulfill such biblical commands and so play your part in building a healthy church. Another way to say it might be, we hope these books will help you grow in loving your church like Jesus loves your church.

9Marks plans to produce a short, readable book on each of what Mark has called nine marks of a healthy church, plus one more on sound doctrine. Watch for books on expositional preaching, biblical theology, the gospel, conversion, evange-lism, church membership, church discipline, discipleship and growth, and church leadership.

Local churches exist to display God's glory to the nations. We do that by fixing our eyes on the gospel of Jesus Christ, trusting him for salvation, and then loving one another with

11

God's own holiness, unity, and love. We pray the book you are holding will help.

With hope,
Mark Dever and Jonathan Leeman
Series editors

FOREWORD

Satan, in his wicked way, is a shrewd strategist. C. S. Lewis reminded us of this in *The Screwtape Letters*, and the apostle Paul clearly never forgot it (e.g. 2 Cor. 2:11; 11:14). Sherlock Holmes spoke of Professor Moriarty as the "Napoleon of crime," and we do well to think of Satan as the "Napoleon of sin." Satan stays active, keeping pace with God, cunningly aiming to spoil God's work and to thwart his plans to do good for his people and bring praise to his name. So the church must ever be at war with Satan, since Satan is always at war with it—with us who believe.

Today, God is renewing within the church a concern for a deeper knowledge of his truth in Scripture and of his love in Christ. Yet already it is observable that Satan seeks to derail this concern by causing trouble in the congregations that possess it. We can be certain, moreover, that he will keep on doing this as long as the renewal of orthodoxy continues. And so books that call for authentic, Christ-centered faith to show itself in Christlike beauty of life—books like this one—become very significant for the Christian cause at this time.

It seems beyond question that we believers do not think often enough, or hard enough, about the culture of our congregations. *Culture*, a word borrowed from sociology, means the public lifestyle that expresses a shared mindset and convictions held in common. A church's culture should be orthopraxy expressing orthodoxy. It should look like self-giving love for others that in turn reflects the sacrificial love for us of Jesus Christ our Savior and our Lord.

By hammering home the reality of this, our cultural calling, and reminding us that Christian belief minus Christian culture is real hypocrisy, Dr. Ortlund renders us good and needed service. May his words be heard and taken to heart.

J. I. Packer
Board of Governors' Professor of Theology
Regent College

INTRODUCTION

Evangelion (what we call "the gospel") is a Greek word, signifying good, merry, glad and joyful news, that makes a man's heart glad and makes him sing, dance and leap for joy.[1]

William Tyndale

William Tyndale, the pioneer translator of the Bible into English, wrote those delightful words in 1525. And he sealed them with a martyr's death. What a world we live in, that something so happy would be so hated! But so it is.

As Tyndale pointed out, the very form of the Greek word translated "gospel" means good news.[2] The gospel is not law, demanding that we pay our own way. The gospel is a welcome announcement, declaring that Jesus paid it all. It's like a long-awaited telephone call. When the phone finally rings, we grab the phone and eagerly take that call. This gospel is a message to be proclaimed and believed (Mark 1:14–15). It is the point of the whole Bible (Gal. 3:8). It comes from God above (Gal. 1:11–12). It is worthy of our utmost (Phil. 1:27–30).

This good news is more than good vibes. This message has specific content. It can and must be defined, and from the Bible alone. Every generation must pick up their Bibles and rediscover the gospel afresh for themselves and rearticulate the ancient message in their own words for their own times.

We are in just such a time of active gospel rediscovery, and it is exciting to be involved.

Here is the essential message Bible-believing people rally around:

> God, through the perfect life, atoning death, and bodily resurrection of Jesus Christ, rescues all his people from the wrath of God into peace with God, with a promise of the full restoration of his created order forever—all to the praise of the glory of his grace.

Salvation from the judgment of God into fellowship with God is all of God. It is not of us. That is good news indeed! And this gospel is widely known and sincerely preached in our churches today.

SOMETHING TROUBLING

But here is something troubling. If a message so good lies at the defining center of our churches, why do we see such bad things in those same churches—ranging from active strife to sheer exhaustion? Where is the saving power of the gospel? Why don't we see more of Tyndale's singing, dancing, and leaping for joy in our churches, if the good news is setting the tone?

In his prophetic book *Witness*, Whittaker Chambers tells of a young German woman whose father had been fervently pro-Communist. Then he became strongly anti-Communist. Why? She said: "You will laugh at me, but you must not laugh at my father. One night, in Moscow, he heard screams. That's all. Simply one night he heard screams."[3]

This happens in our churches too. People come to hear good news. But then they hear screams. They hear cries of anguish and distress in churches that preach the gospel in concept but inflict pain in reality. That is shocking, but it is not new. The prophet Isaiah writes:

> The vineyard of the LORD Almighty
>> is the house of Israel,
> and the men of Judah
>> are the garden of his delight.
> And he looked for justice, but saw bloodshed;
>> for righteousness, but heard cries of distress.
>> (Isa. 5:7, NIV)

How many people in our cities are ex-Christians, and even strongly anti-Christian, because they went to church to hear "good news of great joy" (Luke 2:10) but it was drowned out by strife and trouble?

Let's not assume that our churches are faithful to the gospel. Let's examine whether they are. After all, "Every institution tends to produce its opposite."[4] A church with the truth of the gospel in its theology can produce the opposite of the gospel in its practice. The risen Lord said to one of his churches, "You say, I am rich, I have prospered, and I need nothing, not realizing that you are wretched, pitiable, poor, blind and naked" (Rev. 3:17). The problem was not what they believed doctrinally but what they had become personally, and they didn't even realize it. Yet it was obvious to the Lord: "I know your works" (Rev. 3:15). Therefore, they needed to go to Christ with a new humility, openness, and honesty.

THE TEST OF A GOSPEL-CENTERED CHURCH

Not long after his life-altering crisis of faith, brought on by the personal ugliness he saw in his denomination, Francis Schaeffer wrote an article entitled "How Heresy Should Be Met." Here is his main point:

> The final problem is not to prove men wrong but to win them back to Christ. Therefore, the only ultimately successful apologetic is, first, a clear, intellectual statement of what is wrong with the false doctrine, *plus* a clear, intellectual return to the proper scriptural emphasis, in all its vitality and in its relation to the total Christian Faith, *plus* a demonstration in the life that this correct and vital scriptural emphasis meets the genuine needs and aspirations of men in a way that Satan's counterfeit does not.[5]

So the test of a gospel-centered church is its doctrine on paper *plus* its culture in practice—"a demonstration in the life that this correct and vital scriptural emphasis meets the genuine needs and aspirations of men." If a church's gospel culture has been lost, or was never built, the only remedy is found at the feet of Christ. That church needs a fresh rediscovery of his gospel in all its beauty. It needs to prayerfully reconsider everything it believes and practices. Nothing is gained by merely repackaging the church in forms more attractive to outsiders.

First and foremost, the gospel of Christ must be fully believed and embraced by our churches. That is more profound than a momentary upsurge of enthusiasm. *The need of our times is nothing less than the re-Christianization of our churches, according to the gospel alone, in both doctrine and culture, by*

Christ himself. Nothing less than the beauty of Christ will suffice today, though what a renewed church will look like might, at present, lie beyond our imaginations.

THE PURPOSE OF THIS BOOK

The purpose of this book, then, is simple. I want to show how Christ puts his beauty into our churches by his gospel. That explains the title of this book: *The Gospel: How the Church Portrays the Beauty of Christ.* Beauty is powerful. Our churches long for it. You and I long for it. And we can help our churches see it. We possess, in the gospel alone, God's wonder-working resources for the display of Christ among us. And as you read, I hope you find yourself thrilled with the beauty of Christ. That's my ultimate goal.

So this is a book about the gospel, yes. But more specifically, it's about how the gospel can shape the life and culture of our churches so that they portray Christ as he really is, according to his gospel.

I believe that A. W. Tozer's ironic quip from a generation ago still holds: "A widespread revival of the kind of Christianity we know today in America might prove to be a moral tragedy from which we would not recover in a hundred years."[6] What is there in our churches that *deserves* to survive? What is there in our churches that *can* survive? Any church of any denomination today that falls short of the gospel of Christ in either doctrine or culture will inevitably collapse under the extreme pressures of our times.

My own dear dad said in a sermon years ago, "Only an awakened church . . . only people in a revived condition are going to make a dent on this society."[7] The gospel alone works with the power of God (Rom. 1:16). Everything else, everything less, will be swept away, and rightly so.

Let's set all lesser things aside and prayerfully, before the Lord, rediscover his powerful gospel, while we still can.

1

THE GOSPEL FOR YOU

> For God so loved the world, that he gave his only
> Son, that whoever believes in him should not
> perish but have eternal life.
>
> John 3:16

Gospel doctrine creates a gospel culture. The doctrine of grace creates a culture of grace.

When the doctrine is clear and the culture is beautiful, that church will be powerful. But there are no shortcuts to getting there. Without the doctrine, the culture will be weak. Without the culture, the doctrine will seem pointless.

Gospel doctrine with gospel culture is prophetic. Francis Schaeffer wrote:

> One cannot explain the explosive dynamite, the *dunamis*, of the early church apart from the fact that they practiced two things simultaneously: orthodoxy of doctrine and orthodoxy of community in the midst of the visible church, a community which the world could see. By the grace of God, therefore, the church must be known simultaneously for its purity of doctrine and the reality of its community. Our churches have so often been only preaching points with very little emphasis on community, but exhibition of the love of God in practice is beautiful and must be there.[1]

Schaeffer's words "by the grace of God" are crucial. We need strength from beyond ourselves, because it's hard to hold on to gospel doctrine. It's even harder to create a gospel culture, one so humane and so attractive that people *want* to be part of it. Schaeffer also wrote: "If the church is what it should be, young people will be there. But they will not just 'be there'—they will be there with the blowing of horns and the clashing of high-sounding cymbals, and they will come dancing with flowers in their hair."[2]

We accept that the truth of biblical doctrine is essential to authentic Christianity, but do we accept that the beauty of human relationships is *equally* essential? If by God's grace we hold the two together—gospel doctrine and gospel culture—people of all ages will more likely come to our churches with great joy. It is more likely that they will think, "Here is the answer I've been looking for all my life."

DOCTRINE OR CULTURE?

Every one of us is wired to lean one way or the other—toward emphasizing doctrine or culture. Some of us naturally resonate with truth and standards and definitions. Others of us resonate with feel and vibe and relationships. Whole churches, too, can emphasize one or the other.

Left to ourselves, we will get it partly wrong, but we won't feel wrong, because we'll be partly right. But only partly. Truth without grace is harsh and ugly. Grace without truth is sentimental and cowardly. The living Christ is full of grace and truth (John 1:14). We cannot represent him, therefore, within the limits of our own personalities and backgrounds. Yet as we depend on him moment by moment, both personally and corporately, he will give us wisdom. He will stretch us and make our churches more like himself, so that we can glorify him more clearly than we ever have before.

These equations help me define the matter more simply:

Gospel doctrine – gospel culture = hypocrisy
Gospel culture – gospel doctrine = fragility
Gospel doctrine + gospel culture = power

Only the powerful presence of the risen Lord can make a church this gospel-centered.

Several years ago, author Anne Rice said, "Christians have lost credibility in America as people who know how to love."[3] There might be many reasons for that negative assessment, not all of them convincing. But I cannot dismiss her comment. Neither does the problem that she highlights register as a low priority in the Bible, one we might get around to someday. In fact, few things are more urgent for us than to regain credibility as people who know how to love, for Jesus's sake, so that his glorious gospel is unmistakably clear in our churches.

People will see *him* in *us* as we build our churches into gospel cultures with the resources of gospel doctrine, taking no shortcuts.

John 3:16, perhaps the most famous verse in all the Bible, spreads before us the doctrine of the gospel. This verse is the gospel for you and me personally. The renewal of our churches starts deep within each of us, as we are renewed in the gospel ourselves. So let's think through this wonderful verse, phrase by phrase.

FOR GOD SO LOVED THE WORLD

The gospel is good news, and these momentous words have to be the best news: "For God so loved the world . . ." (John 3:16a). Yet for this verse to make the impact on us it deserves, we must understand two things: who this God is and how he loves this world.

First, who is this God? The word *God* is so familiar to us that we might gloss over it. But we need to think about it. Not one of us has ever had a single thought about God that was fully fair to the magnitude of who he really is. Who *is* the God of the Christian gospel?

A contrast can help. In his book *What Is the Gospel?*, Greg Gilbert uses satire to help us see how we naturally diminish our concept of "God":

Let me introduce you to god. (Note the lowercase *g*.)

You might want to lower your voice a little before we go in. He might be sleeping now. He's old, you know, and doesn't much understand or like this "newfangled" modern world. His golden days—the ones he talks about when you really get him going—were a long time ago, before most of us were even born. That was back when people cared what he thought about things, and considered him pretty important to their lives.

Of course all that's changed now, though, and god—poor fellow—just never adjusted very well. Life's moved on and passed him by. Now, he spends most of his time just hanging in the garden out back. I go there sometimes to see him, and there we tarry, walking and talking softly and tenderly among the roses. . . .

Anyway, a lot of people still like him, it seems—or at least he manages to keep his poll numbers pretty high. And you'd be surprised how many people even drop by to visit and ask for things every once in a while. But of course that's alright with him. He's here to help.

Thank goodness, all the crankiness you read about sometimes in his old books—you know, having the earth swallow people up, raining fire down on cities, that sort of thing—all that seems to have faded in his old age. Now he's just a good-natured, low-maintenance friend who's really easy to talk to—especially since he almost never talks back, and when he does, it's usually to tell me through some slightly weird "sign" that what I want to do regardless is alright by him. That really is the best kind of friend, isn't it?

You know the best thing about him, though? He doesn't judge me. Ever, for anything. Oh sure, I know that deep down he wishes I'd be better—more loving, less selfish, and all that—but he's realistic. He knows I'm human and nobody's perfect. And I'm totally sure he's fine with that. Besides, forgiving people is his job. It's what he *does*. After all, he's love, right? And I like to think of love as "never judging, only forgiving." That's the god *I* know. And I wouldn't have him any other way. . . .

Okay, we can go in now. And don't worry, we don't have to stay long. Really. He's grateful for any time he can get.[4]

Is there anything in Gilbert's picture that reflects how *we* think of God? Let's be honest with ourselves about this.

John Piper helps us all take our spiritual temperatures this way:

For many, Christianity has become the grinding out of general doctrinal laws from collections of biblical facts. But childlike wonder and awe have died. The scenery and poetry and music of the majesty of God have dried up like a forgotten peach at the back of the refrigerator.[5]

In other words, we might affirm the right doctrines, but every one of us still needs to say: "Search me, O God, and know my heart! Try me and know my thoughts!" (Ps. 139:23).

Let's forget everything else for a moment. Let's think about God, because "what comes into our minds when we think about God is the most important thing about us."[6] God does not gain by our clarity about him. We do.

Go all the way back to the beginning. Where did you get your idea of God? And how do you know you didn't make it up?

The gospel displays God gloriously, far beyond what we naturally think, even opposite to what we naturally think. For instance, early in the Bible, God says, "I am God Almighty" (Gen. 17:1). Almost no one believes that God is truly almighty, which is why God said it. But when that amazing thought about God drops into our mental pool, the ripples move out in all directions. Here is what God Almighty reveals to us about himself:

> I am the Almighty God, able to fulfill your highest hopes and accomplish for you the brightest ideal that ever my words set before you. There is no need of paring down the promise until it squares with human probabilities, no need of relinquishing one hope it has begotten, no need of adopting some interpretation of it which may make it seem easier to fulfill, and no need of striving to fulfill it in any second-rate way. All possibility lies in this: I am the Almighty God.[7]

Without this real and glorious God, the task of our lives would be to keep adjusting our expectations of life downward.

Author Reynolds Price understands how dark reality becomes without an almighty God: "There is no Creator and there never was. The universe is pure unillumined matter where senseless atoms and vicious creatures stage the awful pageants of their wills."[8] But with John 3:16 showing us the love of God Almighty, we never have to swallow such hopelessness.

The Christian gospel does not ask us to settle for something. It begins with the almighty God, who, amazingly, doesn't despise the world but loves the world. That's who God really is. It's what the Bible says. Let's believe it.

Now to the second question—how does God love this world? John says, "For God *so* loved the world." The little word *so* is worth noticing. It communicates the intensity of God's love. How did God love the world? Not moderately, but massively. God *so* loved the world, not because we are lovable but because he *is* love (1 John 4:16).

The intense nature of God's love becomes all the more evident when we think about this world of ours that is *so* loved by God. As we grow in seeing God more clearly, we also grow in seeing ourselves more clearly. John observes: "This is the judgment: the light has come into the world, and people loved the darkness rather than the light because their works were evil. For everyone who does wicked things hates the light and does not come to the light" (John 3:19–20). It's hard to admit that we love the darkness, but we know it's true. We have all done evil things and then covered them up, fearing exposure. We've tried to forget the memory and to ignore conscience and to medicate the pain. It is hard for us to face ourselves honestly.

W. H. Auden, in his poem "September 1, 1939," points

to something of this darkness in our individual lives. He describes what he saw one evening in a nightclub:

> Faces along the bar
> Cling to their average day;
> The lights must never go out,
> The music must always play . . .
> Lest we should see where we are,
> Lost in a haunted wood,
> Children afraid of the night
> Who have never been happy or good.[9]

We all see ourselves in this poem, don't we?

John's words about loving the darkness also help us to see ourselves at another level—as a culture. One of the marks of our times is that we redefine evil things as good. We change the labels, as if that could change the realities. We tell ourselves we're better than we really are. This too is "[loving] the darkness rather than the light."

Recently I did a search at Amazon.com for "self-esteem," and I got 93,059 results. Time after time, we have been told that self-regard is how we become well-adjusted and successful people. But is it true?

In her *New York Times* article "The Trouble with Self-Esteem," Lauren Slater quotes a researcher who studied criminals and concluded: "The fact is, we've put antisocial men through every self-esteem test we have, and there's no evidence for the old psychodynamic concept that they secretly feel bad about themselves. These men are racist or violent because they don't feel bad enough about themselves."[10]

The Bible challenges the self-flattery that we cling to in our world today. How? First, the law of God exposes the fraudulence of our virtue by showing us the true holiness of God. We don't deserve as much as we think we do. Second, the Bible simply changes the subject to how much God loves the undeserving. In other words, the gospel helps us to stop barricading ourselves against God, because it's evil people in denial whom God loves so massively.

But we must trust him and open up. After all, we know how dishonesty paralyzes our human relationships. For instance, a friend wrongs you and then pretends it never happened. As a result, the friendship cools, the distance between you grows, and soon there is guardedness where before there was spontaneity. At some point, you realize that what makes the relationship impossible isn't the original wrong but the denial of the wrong.

Our willful denial of God is *the* mega-offense above all our other offenses that God challenges by his massive love in Christ. Our world thinks it is too good for God. It's too touchy and defensive to accept his love. But that does not stop God.

What if it did? What if God said: "So, that's the way you want it? Then have it your way. You hate the light. You love the darkness. Your whole approach to life is to sin and then fake happiness. You refuse to be honest. Okay. But you cannot cling to your self-created falsehood and have my massive love too. This relationship is over forever"? He has the right to say this. Who could blame him if he did!

But what did God do instead?

THAT HE GAVE HIS ONLY SON

God so loved the world "that he gave his only Son." This Son is Jesus, the promised Messiah of the Old Testament and the One who fulfills the deepest hopes of the human heart. The word *only* means that Jesus is unique. There is no other like him. He is therefore irreplaceable. There is no other Savior. The world has no other hope. No one else will appear out of heaven to come rescue us. It's either God's only Son or despair now and damnation forever.

Have you considered the audacious things Jesus says about himself? Here are a few, for starters:

- "I and the Father are one" (John 10:30).
- "Believe in God; believe also in me" (John 14:1).
- "Unless you believe I am he you will die in your sins" (John 8:24).

C. S. Lewis helps us get right to the point:

I am trying here to prevent anyone saying the really foolish thing that people often say about Him: "I'm ready to accept Jesus as a great moral teacher, but I don't accept His claim to be God." That is the one thing we must not say. A man who was merely a man and said the sort of things Jesus said would not be a great moral teacher. He would either be a lunatic . . . or else he would be the Devil of Hell. You must make your choice. Either this man was, and is, the Son of God, or else a madman or something worse. You can shut Him up for a fool, you can spit at Him and kill Him as a demon, or you can fall at His feet and call Him Lord and God. But let us not come with any patronizing nonsense about His being a great human teacher. He has not left that open to us. He did not intend to.[11]

The only Son, given from the massively loving heart of the Father, came into this world "not by constraint but willingly, not with a burning sense of wrong but with a grateful sense of high privilege and . . . a blessed consciousness of fellowship with His Father who sent Him."[12] We did not make him up as a new religion. He came down from God as the archetypal new man, our better self, our only future. He lived the worthy life we have never lived and he died the guilty death we don't want to die. By his life, death, and resurrection, Jesus fulfilled every demand of God in our place. He atoned for our guilt. He satisfied the wrath of God against us. He conquered death on our behalf. He did all that as our substitute, because in our helplessness we could never dig our own way out. God gave us his Son fully, without holding back at all. God even gave him *up* at the cross. He abandoned him to the desolation of the hell we utterly deserve, so that forever and ever he would give us heavenly things we cannot deserve (Rom. 8:32).

This is the massive love of God—the Son leaving nothing of the Father's glory unexpressed, leaving nothing of our need unfilled, opening up the mighty heart of God to the unworthy. But this massive love is laser-focused. The only Son is our only entry point back to God, the only One given by God, the only One acceptable to God. *There is no other.* I dare you to name one other hope in all this world of which this can be said:

> The obedience and death of the Lord Jesus laid the foundation
> and opened the way for the exercise of this great and sover-
> eign act of grace. The cross of Jesus displays the most awesome

exhibition of God's hatred of sin, and at the same time the most august manifestation of his readiness to pardon it. Pardon, full and free, is written out in every drop of blood that is seen, is proclaimed in every groan that is heard . . . . Oh blessed door of return, open and never shut, to the wanderer from God! How glorious, how free, how accessible! Here the sinful, the vile, the guilty, the unworthy, the poor, the penniless, may come. Here too the weary spirit may bring its burden, the broken spirit its sorrow, the guilty spirit its sin, the backsliding spirit its wandering. All are welcome here. The death of Jesus was the opening and the emptying of the full heart of God. It was the outgushing of that ocean of infinite mercy that heaved and panted and longed for an outlet. It was God showing *how* he could love a poor, guilty sinner. What more could he have done than this?[13]

Every other hope is based, explicitly or implicitly, on how deserving we are. Only the Christian gospel is based—clearly, boldly, and insistently—on how loving God is to the undeserving. If you thought you could earn, demand, and fight your way through life on the basis of your own entitlements and cleverness, but now you find within yourself not light but darkness and denial, not freedom but impasse; if you have shocked yourself with the evil you're capable of and have given up on yourself in despair, the God of love waits for you with open arms today.

When we finally abandon our pretenses and open up to the love of God, we always find it right where God himself put it—in his only Son. In Christ alone, we, the guilty, will find all the love that we will ever need. That is what the gospel says.

But how do we get there?

THAT WHOEVER BELIEVES WON'T PERISH BUT HAVE LIFE

John concludes verse 16 with the answer: "that whoever believes in him should not perish but have eternal life." The word *whoever* is broad. Anyone, however discredited, can enter in. At the same time, the words *not perish but have eternal life* are narrow. Perishing and eternal life are the only alternatives standing before us. Every one of us will go one way or the other. It all depends on whether we will "believe in him," the only Son of God.

What then does it mean to believe in him? Here is what it does *not* mean. In English, we might say, "I believe in the free-enterprise system," that is to say, "I agree with it, I like it." But try that out on John 3:16: "For God so loved this evil world, that he gave the sacrificial gift of his only Son, so that we could say, 'Sure, that's what I believe in—along with Motherhood and Apple Pie.'" The massive love of God calls for more and creates more than mild agreement.

The Greek text of John 3:16 literally says, "whoever believes *into* him should not perish." Real belief takes us *into* Jesus Christ. Real belief destroys aloofness. It moves us from self-completeness into Christ-completeness. We stop treating him as a religious garnish to be placed on the side of life. Rather, we find in him our all. He becomes our new sacred center. We gladly lose ourselves in who he is for desperate sinners. Theologians call this radical reorientation "union with Christ." It's that profound.

When I believe into Christ, I stop hiding and resisting. I surrender my autonomy. In response to the good news of all that Jesus has done, I hurl myself at him as my only hope. I want to be *really* forgiven of my *real* sins by a *real* Savior.

When you look at Jesus in this new way, the Bible says you are brought safely *into* him forever. How wonderful! You can never be forsaken there, because all forsakenness landed on the cross, far away from us. His grace, received by faith and not works, relocates you deeply into his heart.

Gerhard Forde helps us accept the simplicity of believing as opposed to earning:

> We are justified freely, for Christ's sake, by faith, without the exertion of our own strength, gaining of merit, or doing of works. To the age-old question, "What shall I do to be saved?" the confessional answer is shocking: "Nothing! Just be still; shut up and listen for once in your life to what God the Almighty, creator and redeemer, is saying to his world and to you in the death and resurrection of his Son! Listen and believe!"[14]

What matters most to God is not which sins we've committed or not committed, or how we stack up in comparison with other sinners. What matters most to God is whether we've bonded by faith with his only Son. In other words, God's final category for you is not your goodness *versus* your badness, but your union with Christ *versus* your distance from Christ. To put it yet another way, what matters most about you in God's sight is not the bad or good things you've done but your trust and openness to Christ *versus* your self-trust and defensiveness toward Christ.

God has simplified everything for everyone. We don't have to be good enough. We don't have to know all the answers. God has the answers. He has lovingly provided everything in Christ. There is no reason for us to hold back. Why remain cool and guarded when God offers his massive love in the most obviously wonderful person who ever walked the face of the earth? Why not trust him? If you do, he will draw you in, and he will do so forever. This is the promise of the gospel.

If you don't believe your way into Jesus Christ, you will perish.

Do you see that word *perish* in John 3:16? Stare at it for a while. It's captured dimly in a play called *Breath*, written in 1969 by Samuel Beckett, who contributed to that era's "theater of the absurd" movement. The whole play lasts about thirty-five seconds. The curtains part to reveal a pile of garbage on stage. There are no actors. The only sound is a human cry as the lights come up, which is followed by silence, which is followed by a whimper as the lights go out. End of play, end of life, end of story. That is a picture of perishing—a lifetime that leaves behind a trail of cast-off clothes, old computers, carbon emissions, and lost opportunities, then a funeral, and then the death of everyone who wept at your funeral. You don't matter ever again, except when you stand before the white-hot judgment of God in eternity, where you will give an account for rejecting him. Hell is for people who could have enjoyed the love of God but held back. The Bible says, "They will suffer the punishment of eternal destruction, away from the presence of the Lord" (2 Thess. 1:9). That is perishing.

But eternal life is available right now to hell-deserving sinners massively loved by the all-glorious God who gave his only Son. The only thing he asks is that we respond to that good news by turning from ourselves and receiving Christ with the empty hands of faith. Have you trusted in him? Have you forsaken yourself and turned to him as your complete Savior? Will you do so right now? He offers and promises eternal life, in himself, to all who simply believe.

Jonathan Edwards helps us to become decisive for Christ:

> What is there that you could desire in a Savior that is not in Christ? . . . What is there that is great or good, what is there that is venerable or winning, what is there that is adorable or endearing, or what can you think of that would be encouraging which is not to be found in the person of Christ? Would you have your Savior to be great and honorable, because you are unwilling to be beholden to a low person? And is not Christ honorable enough to be worthy that you should be dependent on him? Is he not a person high enough to be appointed to so honorable a work as your salvation? Would you not only have a Savior of high degree but would you have him . . . to be made also of low degree, that he might experience afflictions and trials, that he might learn by the things that he has suffered, to pity those who suffer and are tempted? And has not Christ been made low enough for you, and has he not suffered enough? . . . What is there lacking, or what would you add if you could, to make Christ more fit to be your Savior?[15]

FROM DOCTRINE TO CULTURE

The love of God in Christ is the breathtaking doctrine of John 3:16. Now here is the beautiful church culture called for by that doctrine: "Beloved, if God *so* loved us, we also ought to love one another" (1 John 4:11).

Peter puts it this way: "Love one another earnestly"

(1 Pet. 1:22). We are not to love moderately but earnestly, the way God loves.

There is a lot of love in this world, most of it moderate. But under the blessing of God, gospel doctrine cracks our hearts open to receive something from beyond this world. We see how massive God's love really is, and so we give up our aloofness and come together to care for one another in real ways, even as God wonderfully cares for us. That is when a church starts looking like a community where the God of John 3:16 dwells in power. That is when the world can see his love in reality, and many will join us in Christ and live forever.

Gospel doctrine creates a gospel culture, and it matters.

2

THE GOSPEL FOR
THE CHURCH

Christ loved the church and gave himself up for her.

Ephesians 5:25

The doctrine of grace creates a culture of grace where good things happen to bad people. A gracious church culture proves that Jesus is the Holy One who forgives sinners, the King who befriends his enemies, the Genius who counsels failures.

Gospel doctrine and gospel culture do not coexist by lucky chance. The doctrine creates and sustains the culture. The way we live together in our churches grows out of what we believe together. So the gospel must land on each of us personally. You and I must believe the gospel for ourselves, first and foremost. But the gospel also creates a new kind of community—a gospel culture called a church.

What is a church? A church—not *the* church but *a* church—is a body of believers in Jesus, together drawing their life from him in regular, practical, organized ways that accelerate their progress for him.[1] You and I are one with all true Christians throughout history—Augustine, Martin

Luther, Johann Sebastian Bach, and many other amazing people. That's exciting. But the unity of the church becomes our actual experience in the unity of a church. In our local churches, what we share goes beyond our experiences with Christians in general. Being part of a church frees us from a vague idealism and gives us traction for real gospel advance that will matter forever.

Your church is more than a collection of people who happen to get together on Sundays. You could go to a professional football game on a Sunday afternoon for a mere get-together. The fans of a team might sit together, wear the team colors, and cheer in unison when their team scores. But when the game is over, they walk out of the stadium, drive home, and get on with their separate lives. You could even attend a big Christian event for a mere get-together. There might be wonderful magic in the air, but does anything *corporate* last once the event is over and everyone walks out?

Let's say you meet someone at that Christian event. You really like the person. Two weeks later you happen to run into that person at a coffee shop. That's heartwarming. But it isn't a gospel culture. It is only in a church that we are *members* of Christ and of one another, moving forward together like a well-coordinated body (1 Cor. 12:12–27). It is together that we suffer and thrive. It is together that we worship and grow and serve, according to the Word of God. That's what your church is—ground zero for the new kind of *community* Christ is creating in the world today for the display of his glory. That is a gospel culture.

Obviously, we pay a price to give our lives to a real community. We lose some of our space, time, and freedom to do as we please. But the Bible tells us to submit to one another (Eph. 5:21). That requires us to adjust, to fit in, to always look for the win/win.

So let me ask you a simple question: To whom do you submit? Every one of us should have a good answer to that. The Bible goes so far as to say, "Respect those who . . . are *over you in the Lord*" (1 Thess. 5:12).

Scripture is clear. Christians have to choose between isolation, which is easy, and belonging, which is costly—and much more satisfying.[2]

Here is why our belonging to a church matters so much to God. We are living stones in the spiritual temple that he is building in the world today (1 Pet. 2:4–5). He wants to dwell *among his people*, and we as living stones find ourselves when we are built into the spiritual temple.[3] There is no churchless Christianity in the Bible. We individualistic Americans need to face that. God is building a new *community*, and it's worth belonging to.

In John 3:16, we saw that God so loved the world in general that he gave his only Son. In Ephesians 5:25b–27, we see that Christ loved the church in particular, so that he gave himself for her. That is the gospel doctrine. Let's think about this passage phrase by phrase.

CHRIST LOVED AND DIED FOR THE CHURCH

Paul teaches, "Christ loved the church and gave himself up for her" (Eph. 5:25b). Christ's whole attitude toward his church is love. There has never been a time when he did not love his people with all his mighty heart. John Flavel, a Puritan theologian, imaginatively re-creates the conversation between God the Father and God the Son in eternity past before time began:

> Father: My Son, here is a company of poor miserable souls that have utterly undone themselves and now lie open to my justice. Justice demands satisfaction for them, or will satisfy itself in the eternal ruin of them. What shall be done for these souls?

> Son: O my Father, such is my love to and pity for them that rather than they shall perish eternally, I will be responsible for them as their Guarantee. Bring all your bills, that I may see what they owe you. Lord, bring them all in, that there may be no after-reckonings with them. At my hand you will require it. I would rather choose to suffer your wrath than they suffer it. Upon me, my Father, upon me be all their debt.

> Father: But my Son, if you undertake for them, you must pay the last penny. Expect no discounts. If I spare them, I will not spare you.

> Son: I am willing, Father. Let it be so. Charge it all to me. I am able to pay their debt. And though it will undo me, though it will impoverish all my riches and empty all my accounts, yet I am content to undertake it.[4]

We didn't ruin God's plan; we *are* his plan, his eternal plan to love the undeserving, for the display of his glory alone. In accordance with his loving plan, Christ then gave himself up for his church at the cross. All the wrath of God against the church's sins was forever exhausted in Christ crucified. He gave himself so utterly that he paid the last penny of our debt. He cleared us completely, though it cost him completely. Therefore, for Jesus's sake alone, God's approval now smiles upon his church.

TO SANCTIFY AND CLEANSE HER WITH THE WORD

Yet it's not as though we were attractive. Christ saw us, and sees us, as we really are—unclean. Why did he give himself up for this unattractive church? Paul continues: "that he might sanctify her, [cleansing[5]] her by the washing of water with the word" (Eph. 5:26).

Christ's eternal love and sacrificial death had a purpose: to sanctify the church. That is, he purposed to consecrate us, to set us apart to himself. His love is too great to have allowed us to go on with self-centered lives. Therefore, he took possession of us for a holy purpose, and we no longer belong to ourselves. He took us from the gutter and claimed us for himself. The word *sanctify* fills us with new dignity. We can stand tall now and not grovel anymore. We belong to Christ the Savior, and to no other. How could it be otherwise?

In the context of Ephesians 5, this love of Christ is *marital* in nature. And our new marriage to him, our union with him alone, is not the result of our heroic choice of him but of his merciful choice of us.

When men look for a bride, they often look for a beauty queen. But Christ chose the dirty one who needed his cleansing. The Son of God crossed the tracks to the wrong side of town, where we all live, to find his bride. We brought into the relationship our messy backgrounds, our ongoing problems, and our shame. But we can face all of that now because of what he brought into the relationship: cleansing enough for all our dirty guilt.

How does he cleanse his bride? He does it "by the washing of water with the word." Some interpreters take this as a reference to baptism. That might be included. But it seems more likely that Paul is thinking of the total ministry of the gospel in our churches.[6] The Bible says, "You were washed, you were sanctified, you were justified in the name of the Lord Jesus Christ and by the Spirit of our God" (1 Cor. 6:11). What, then, is Ephesians 5:26 saying? The Lord, having claimed us for himself, makes his love real as the gospel word washes over us Sunday after Sunday. That is how he refreshes us and makes his churches fit for himself. There is nothing degrading in Christ, nothing we need to worry about or filter out. His eternal love rains down on us in our churches with renewing power through the ministry of gospel words (see Isa. 55:10–11).

The prophet Ezekiel also saw God as the husband of his people (Ezekiel 16). He saw the young nation of Israel as an abandoned baby girl, unwashed and unloved. Then God came by. His heart went out to her. He cared for her. He bathed, clothed, and raised her. She became beautiful. He married her and adorned her.

"But," God then said to his people, "you trusted in your beauty and played the whore because of your renown and lavished your whorings on any passerby" (Ezek. 16:15). This statement is disturbing. What is the Lord talking about? He is declaring a hard but important truth. Whenever our sinful hearts don't find the love of our divine Husband satisfying, and we take our anxiety, loneliness, or needs to other remedies and comforts that leave God out, we commit spiritual adultery. Who of us has not done that? We are all whores many times over. The gospel is not the story of Christ loving a pure bride who loves him; it's the story of his love for a whore who thinks he has nothing to offer and keeps giving herself to others. Therefore, every church set apart to Christ continues to need a cleansing so great it must come down from above through the ongoing ministry of the Word.

I apologize for putting this so bluntly, but it's in the Bible. We need to face it. How can we hope to be true to Christ if we look away from the Bible's stark portrayal of our natural corruption? The Bible alerts us that a blasphemous attitude lurks in all our hearts. We tell ourselves: "What's the big deal about this or that compromise? He'll understand. He's all about grace, right?" But what man would say: "What's the big deal about my wife's adulteries? It's only marriage. I understand. I'm all about grace"? In the same way, our divine Husband does not think, "Well, she's brought another lover into our bed, but as long as they let me sleep, what's the big deal?" The thought is revolting.

The love of Jesus is sacred. He gives all, and he demands all, because he is a *good* Husband. Only an exclusive love is real love. Only a cleansing grace is real grace. Would we even desire a grace that did not cleanse us for Christ?

Let's give ourselves afresh to our Lord, and to him only, and let's never stop doing so. And let's never stop telling our generation: "We're not saying Jesus is just one way, or even the best way. We're saying he is the *only* way. Come join us in the only real love that exists in all the universe. Get out of the brothel of this world, where everything is for sale and everyone has a price. Come into the eternal marriage, where you will no longer be bought and sold but loved and cherished forever. You can be cleansed of all your whoredoms by the power of his grace. You can have your virginity back, you can have your integrity back, freely given by the love of Christ, constantly refreshed through the gospel of Christ. Come to him!"

So Christ's initial purpose for his church is to claim us and renew us. But there's more.

THAT HE MIGHT PRESENT THE CHURCH IN SPLENDOR

Christ has a still greater purpose for his church. It takes us all the way into eternity future. He died for the church and washes her with the word, Paul says, "so that he might present the church to himself in splendor, without spot or wrinkle or any such thing, that she might be holy and without blemish" (Eph. 5:27). The emphatic words are *he* and *to himself*. *He* will beautify us. *He* will satisfy his own loving heart for us.

The Bible tells us that God is a jealous God (Ex. 34:14). Paul enters into this godly jealousy when he writes to the Corinthian church, "I feel a divine jealousy for you, since I betrothed you to one husband, to present you as a pure virgin to Christ" (2 Cor. 11:2). It should not be surprising, therefore, to see what Paul expects of a church: "a sincere and pure devotion to Christ" (v. 3). If our churches are ever so foolish as to say that Jesus is one among others, if we allow any other passion to interfere with our reverent enjoyment of the Lord Jesus Christ himself, we will defy his loving purpose and corrupt ourselves. The Lord will be able to give us our honor back, but only through our repentance.

Nothing in all this world, however tempting, compares with Christ. Look at the glorious destiny he has for his people. He will present us to himself in *splendor*. On that eternal wedding day above, the bride will not need any makeup (Rev. 21:2). He will look into our eyes and say to us, "My love, you are perfect," and he will not be exaggerating. Real holiness is not dull, drab, and negative. Those are marks of man-made religiosity. The real holiness Christ creates is *beautiful*. And the holiness he gives will redeem every dirty thing we have ever done to ourselves or suffered from others. We will be "without spot or wrinkle or *any* such thing." We will be perfected forever, because we will finally be with him and for him *only*. He will do this. He has promised.

The love of Christ is the greatest power in the universe—far greater than all our sins. John Owen, a Puritan theologian, compares our weak love with his powerful love:

> A man may love another as his own soul, yet his love may not be able to help him. He may pity him in prison, but not relieve him, bemoan him in misery, but not help him, suffer with him in trouble, but not ease him. We cannot love grace into a child, nor mercy into a friend; we cannot love them into heaven, though it may be the greatest desire of our soul. . . . But the love of Christ, being the love of God, is effective and fruitful in producing all the good things which he wills for his beloved.

He loves life, grace and holiness into us; he loves us into covenant, loves us into heaven.[7]

That is the church's gospel doctrine. It cleanses us and renews us.

FROM DOCTRINE TO CULTURE

What about the church's gospel culture? It includes so much, such as the ability to be honest about ourselves and to hope in the love of Christ our Husband. But most of all, a church's gospel culture is marked by a beautiful holiness. It remains imperfect in this life, but it's visible and lovely. Our Lord says to us, "You shall be holy, for I am holy" (1 Pet. 1:16). A new culture of holiness to the Lord flows from deep within—from hearts that are refreshed in the love of Christ and given over to him alone. We might look at our unholiness and think: "I'm no good at this. I will only fail and fail and fail. Therefore, holiness doesn't matter." But the gospel teaches us to think: "I'm no good at this. I do fail and fail and fail. Therefore, the promise of Christ is what matters. *He* will make me holy as he is holy, for his own glory. I will believe the gospel. I will put my trust in the mighty love of Christ."

Here is how we make that trust a practical reality. The Bible says we have been married to the risen Christ in order to bear fruit for God (Rom. 7:4). We're not married to a dead and helpless Jesus but to a living and powerful Jesus. At conversion, what did we do? We gave ourselves to him. We put ourselves in his arms. We surrendered to his love. And we started changing by his power. But as in any healthy marriage, we are to give ourselves to him over and over again. We gave ourselves to him once, and we give ourselves to him constantly, in trust and surrender, moment by moment. Over time, then, he faithfully brings forth his fruit through us.[8] His holiness starts to show only by his miraculous power in our weakness and corruption. Then people can see his beauty in the world today—in churches graced with holiness.

3

THE GOSPEL FOR EVERYTHING

And he who was seated on the throne said, "Behold, I am making all things new."

Revelation 21:5

Gospel doctrine creates gospel cultures called churches, where wonderful things happen to unworthy people for the glory of Christ alone. But it doesn't end in our churches. A gospel-defined church is a prophetic sign that points beyond itself. It is a model home of the new neighborhood Christ is building for eternity.[1] People can walk into this kind of church right now to see human beauty that will last forever. Such a church makes heaven real to people on earth so that they can put their faith in Christ now, while they still have the chance.

Revelation 21 shows us how big the gospel really is. It is as big as the universe. Redemption is as big as creation. How could it be otherwise? The Bible's story starts here: "In the beginning, God created the heavens and the earth" (Gen. 1:1). It ends here: "Then I saw a new heaven and a new earth" (Rev. 21:1).

Lesslie Newbigin points out the significance of how the

Bible begins and ends: "The Bible is unique among the sacred books of the world's religions in that it is in structure a history of the cosmos. It claims to show us the shape, the structure, the origin, and the goal not merely of human history, but of cosmic history."[2]

We need a hope that big. After all, we live in a world that has been "subjected to futility" (Rom. 8:20). We are crippled people in a crippled world, and we experience the pain every day. Bob Dylan sums it up in his typical way:

> Broken bottles, broken plates
> Broken switches, broken gates
> Broken dishes, broken parts
> Streets are filled with broken hearts
> Broken words never meant to be spoken
> Everything is broken.[3]

It's a mercy of God that anything works at all. We sometimes think: "My life is hard. Where is God?" We should be thinking: "My life is livable. Thank you, God." Why don't we all have cancer, AIDS, and diabetes? Why aren't we all plotting to murder one another? Why do we love Jesus at all? There is only one explanation: God is down underneath the mess, holding us all together, moving us steadily toward Christ— "Underneath are the everlasting arms" (Deut. 33:27). The Bible says that at this very moment the Lord Jesus "upholds the universe by the word of his power" (Heb. 1:3). John Calvin comments: "To 'uphold' is used in the sense of to care for and to keep all creation in its proper state. He sees that everything will quickly disintegrate, if it is not upheld by His goodness."[4]

The hope of the gospel is far more than a psychological boost to help us ramp up for Monday morning. Look at the magnitude of what God has promised us:

> For behold, I create new heavens
>   and a new earth,
> and the former things shall not be remembered
>   or come into mind. (Isa. 65:17)

On that great and final day, as we step together into the new creation, you might turn to me and say: "Hey, Ray, I'm trying to remember: did we call it 'cancer'? Was that it? Oh, no matter. Here we go!"

In fact, this divine restoration of the created order, foreseen by the prophets, is not completely ahead of us. The promised future landed in this world two thousand years ago, when Jesus announced that he was starting to fulfill the old prophecies (Luke 4:16–21). This is why Jesus healed people. His healings weren't stunts. They were a preview of coming attractions. I disagree with the theology of Jürgen Moltmann in some ways, but he helps us to see this aspect of reality clearly:

> When Jesus expels demons and heals the sick, he is driving out of creation the powers of destruction, and is healing and restoring created beings who are hurt and sick. The lordship of God, to which the healings witness, restores sick creation to health. Jesus' healings are not supernatural miracles in a natural world. They are the only truly "natural" thing in a world that is unnatural, demonized and wounded. . . . Finally, with the resurrection of Christ, the new creation begins, *pars pro toto*, with the crucified one.[5]

Our Lord's resurrection gives us a glimpse, in one man, of the future redeemed human race. The risen Jesus is a second Adam, a new beginning (1 Cor. 15:45). And we who are believers share in his newness now: "If anyone is in Christ, he is a new creation" (2 Cor. 5:17). Becoming a Christian doesn't just add something to the old you; it creates a new you. The risen Christ indwells you now, never to leave (Rom. 8:10–11).

People who believe this big gospel show it. We still suffer, like others. But we are "sorrowful, yet always rejoicing" (2 Cor. 6:10). We "rejoice in hope of the glory of God" (Rom. 5:2). Each of us is like a homeless man who sleeps under a bridge and eats out of dumpsters. One day a limousine pulls up and out steps an attorney who hands him a letter. A long-lost uncle has died and left him a fortune. The check will arrive in a few days. Suddenly, the cardboard shelter doesn't feel so hopeless. He can live with it for a while longer. A vast fortune is coming.

In the same way, a gospel-rich church rejoices in hope. We are poor sinners who can look beyond present circumstances and enjoy our future by faith right now.

Thanks to Jesus, our existence is glorious even now, and we possess the promise of an eternal glory still to come. How different this is from the popular cynicism of our day. Dorothy Sayers describes this ethos:

> In the world it is called Tolerance, but in hell it is called Despair . . . the sin that believes in nothing, cares for nothing, seeks to know nothing, interferes with nothing, enjoys nothing, hates nothing, finds purpose in nothing, lives for noth-

ing, and remains alive because there is nothing for which it will die.[6]

Despair is an intellectual and social sin. It denies gospel doctrine and destroys gospel culture. But God is creating cultures of hope, expectancy, and good cheer in our churches, so that people can see a glimpse of the future and join in.

Hey, all my Christian friends out there, *we're not going to hell anymore! We're going to heaven forever!*

And heaven will not be singing in mass choirs up in the clouds. Heaven will consist of real people living in a real creation, freed from all evil and misery and renewed in unimaginable beauty, because the Lord will be with us.

This bright gospel has the power to sustain us through our hardships in this world in the same way that a star helped Sam Gamgee in the midst of his difficult journey with Frodo in the *Lord of the Rings* trilogy. Deep in the evil land of Mordor, Sam was looking into the nighttime sky when the clouds parted just a bit:

> Sam saw a white star twinkle for a while. The beauty of it smote his heart, as he looked up out of the forsaken land, and hope returned to him. For like a shaft, clear and cold, the thought pierced him that in the end the Shadow was only a small and passing thing; there was light and high beauty forever beyond its reach.[7]

Revelation 21:1–5 shines like that star in our nighttime sky. The promise of this passage will not go away, however dark the night. Let's look at it.

THEN I SAW A NEW HEAVEN AND EARTH

The passage begins, "Then I saw a new heaven and a new earth, for the first heaven and the first earth had passed away, and the sea was no more" (Rev. 21:1).

This verse does not tell us that God will discard nature; it tells us he will redeem it. The key word here is *new*, occurring four times in the passage (vv. 1, 2, 5). *New* does not mean the universe will be completely new, as if it will bear no continuity with the present universe. It means that this universe, this present heaven and earth, will be renewed. God will restore this creation that he made, owns, and loves—this creation where we ourselves feel at home.

Fixing broken things is the way of God. I heard about an African mother whose child asked her, "What is God doing all day long?" She wisely answered, "Mending broken things."[8] God takes damaged goods like us and brings renewal that can never be undone. There will never be another "fall of Adam" to reverse the newness Jesus creates.

Why does verse 1 say "the sea was no more"? The book of Revelation is highly symbolic, and often the Old Testament explains the symbolism. So it is here. The prophet Isaiah wrote, "But the wicked are like the tossing sea; for it cannot be quiet, and its waters toss up mire and dirt" (Isa. 57:20). Throughout history, the wicked have caused waves of social upheaval, surging with anger and frustration. They are never settled, never at peace. But on that final and eternal day, we will no longer have to worry about wars, riots, assassinations, stock market crashes, hostile takeovers, or degrading social trends. So, this verse is *not* saying there will be no surfing in heaven! Rather, when Christ comes, we will have real world peace.

AND I SAW THE HOLY CITY COMING DOWN FROM HEAVEN

Where will this wonderful new *shalom* come from? It will come from above. John continues: "And I saw the holy city, new Jerusalem, coming down out of heaven from God, prepared as a bride adorned for her husband" (Rev. 21:2).

We should do all the good we can for this world right now. But we will never build heaven on earth. Only God can do that, and he will do it at the second coming of Christ—for his glory alone.

What will God bring down to us? The perfect community. Imagine all the members of your church living together in perfect love, sympathy, righteousness, and understanding. What's more, imagine an even more diverse version of your church— with representatives of every tribe, tongue, and nation—living together in such a way that each considers the other's interests more significant than his or her own. No lying. No posturing. No one-upmanship. But shared rejoicing. Shared laboring. Shared zeal.

The promise of the gospel is not about you going to heaven to be with Jesus alone; the promise is that all of God's people will be with him in glorious community forever. We will be a city, a *new* Jerusalem, the true and eternal dwelling place of God among his people.

Why a city? Partly because heaven *shouldn't* be a city. Cain invented the city as his way of running from God (Gen. 4:17). A man-made city is more than a collection of buildings. It is a mechanism for living without having to depend on God. You can be on your own in a city. You can hide in a city. But what does God do with our strategy for evading him? He turns the city into *heaven*. That's what a Redeemer does!

It will be a holy city. There will be no slums, no garbage, no graffiti, no smog, no dirt and grime, no sin. Las Vegas is sometimes called "Sin City." Deep down, sadly, we all have a taste for sin, so none of us can look down on Las Vegas. But what could God our Redeemer do for Sin City? It's hard to imagine. One thing is for sure: a divinely renewed Las Vegas would not be boring. Boredom is what we create, and then we build evil places such as gambling casinos to offset the boredom. But does it work? Have you seen the people sitting in front of the slot machines, dropping in their coins? Do they look like the people in the commercials—young, good-looking, and having the time of their lives? God's city will not be built on false promises. He is not capable of so disappointing us. His holy city, the New Jerusalem, will satisfy us in ways we've always longed for.

Here is the reason. The holy city will be more than a horizontal community, wonderful as that will be. The holy city will also be a bride adorned for a heavenly Bridegroom (v. 2). The book of Revelation spoke earlier of "the marriage of the Lamb" (Rev. 19:7). This too can be difficult for us to imagine. There are times in life when we can hardly believe Christ loves us, and we hardly love him. But it will not always be so. The promise of the gospel is that our churches will be "adorned for [our] husband." His love will heal our shame and raise us out of unbelief and lethargy. We will love him with a fiery affection, even as he has always loved us intensely with all his mighty heart.

That wonderful day will never end. There will be no post-honeymoon letdown. Forever and ever our total experience will be love between us and our Savior. We will never experience anything else, anything less.

THE DWELLING PLACE OF GOD IS WITH MAN

The glorious promises unfold still further:

> And I heard a loud voice from the throne saying, "Behold, the dwelling place of God is with man. He will dwell with them, and they will be his people, and God himself will be with them as their God. He will wipe away every tear from their eyes, and death shall be no more, neither shall there be mourning, nor crying, nor pain anymore, for the former things have passed away." (Rev. 21:3–4)

There can be so much pain in our lives now—so many regrets, so many tears that no one sees. Under the buffetings of this life, we sometimes wonder: "Can I ever be happy again? Will I ever get my life back? Is my future something I'll just have to settle for?"

But what if these amazing verses are true? What if they describe *our* future in Christ?

The centerpiece is this: "God himself will be with them as their God." A day is coming when we will know God's immediate presence, and his presence will not be one of reproach but of comfort. We will be in his presence not because we have overcome our sin and patched ourselves up, but because Christ took on himself all our sin and sadness, while he gave us his sweet and endless mercies. He will open to us the eternal joys presently hidden in the sacred realities of who God is. That is *the* great promise of the gospel. And it is given to all who believe through the merit of Christ alone. Otherwise, we have to wonder, "How could someone like me have God?" Because of Christ's merit, the real question is, "How could someone like me refuse God?"

My friend, do not refuse God. Is anything keeping you from receiving God as your eternal joy?

In the Old Testament era, God dwelt among his people in the tabernacle and then the temple (Ex. 25:8). God told Solomon that as long as the king obeyed, God would remain among the people (1 Kings 6:11–13). But Solomon and his descendants who succeeded him on the throne disobeyed, so the glory departed (Ezekiel 9–11). Yet even before it departed, the temple walls separated God's presence from God's people.

On the great and endless day promised in Revelation 21, there will be no walls, no separation, no distance, no absence. Instead, there will be direct and personal intimacy with God eternally. In his presence, there will be no pain, no suffering. He will wipe every tear from our eyes. The profound anguish of our sufferings in this life will be fully resolved. We will rise healed and whole, never to weep again.

This is the priceless hope given us in the Bible: "God himself will be with them as their God."

Oh, how we should therefore hate the prosperity gospel and its promise of worldly wealth over and above Jesus! That false gospel insults God as second-rate, a useful steppingstone toward a better job or a bigger house. The prosperity gospel also robs us, taking our hearts away from the only joy we were created for—God himself.

Here is the promise of the true gospel, as Jonathan Edwards describes it:

> There, in heaven, this infinite fountain of love—this eternal Three in One—is set open without any obstacle to hinder access to it. . . . There this glorious God is manifested and shines forth in full glory, in beams of love. And there this glorious fountain forever flows forth in streams, yes, in rivers of love and delight, and these rivers swell, as it were, to an ocean of love, in which the souls of the ransomed may bathe with the sweetest enjoyment, and their hearts will be, as it were, deluged with love![9]

HE IS MAKING ALL THINGS NEW

John concludes this section with a royal decree: "And he who was seated on the throne said, 'Behold, I am making all things new'" (Rev. 21:5).

This is the true magnitude of the biblical gospel: There will be nothing old, dilapidated, impure, or worn out in the radiant kingdom of Christ. We will encounter nothing that has a sad memory associated with it. Everything we experience, every new association and memory, will exponentially increase, purify, and intensify our joy forever, since it all comes from the hand of God.

How can all this happen? Through the One seated on the throne, who will make all things wonderfully new. Who will put an end to war? Who will defeat Satan? Who will bring justice to the nations? Who will repair the damage and wreckage from all our sins? He will—our King, who reigns even now from his throne of grace, to whom be glory forever!

That is the gospel doctrine.

FROM DOCTRINE TO CULTURE

How does this gospel doctrine lead to a gospel culture? It creates churches of bright, resilient, rugged hope. It creates churches that face life as it is and are not defeated.

There is nothing petty and small about a church when it believes this massive and noble gospel. And there is nothing this world can dish out to our churches that our Savior won't bend upward and use to lift us closer to our eternal home. Paul, who knew of this world's hardships as much as anyone, observed: "So we do not lose heart. Though our outer self is wasting away, our inner self is being renewed day by day. For this light momentary affliction is preparing for us an eternal weight of glory beyond all comparison" (2 Cor. 4:16–17).

In the face of everything that would seem to rob us of God, this assurance builds into us *a cheerful defiance*. It does so in two ways.

First, the hope of the gospel makes us cheerfully defiant toward every disappointment that we endure in this broken world. Augustine teaches us:

> You are surprised that the world is losing its grip, that the world is grown old? Think of a man: he is born, he grows up, he becomes old. Old age has its many complaints: coughing, shaking, failing eyesight, anxious, terribly tired. A man grows old; he is full of complaints. The world is old; it is full of pressing tribulations.... Do not hold onto the old man, the world; do not refuse

to regain your youth in Christ, who says to you, "The world is passing away, the world is losing its grip, the world is short of breath. Do not fear. Thy youth shall be renewed as an eagle."[10]

Second, the hope of the gospel and the triumph of our Savior make us cheerfully defiant even toward our own sins and failures. Martin Luther teaches us:

When the devil throws our sins up to us and declares that we deserve death and hell, we ought to speak thus: "I admit that I deserve death and hell. What of it? Does this mean that I shall be sentenced to eternal damnation? By no means. For I know One who suffered and made satisfaction in my behalf. His name is Jesus Christ, the Son of God. Where he is, there I shall be also."[11]

4

SOMETHING NEW

I hope to come to you soon, but I am writing
these things to you so that, if I delay, you may
know how one ought to behave in the household of God, which is the church of the living
God, a pillar and buttress of the truth.

1 Timothy 3:14–15

We have surveyed the gospel message at three levels—the good news for ourselves, for the church, and for creation. Now let's press further into the implications for our churches. Specifically, what does the gospel create in this present world that wasn't here before?

The gospel does not hang in midair as an abstraction. By the power of God, the gospel creates something new in the world today. It creates not just a new community, but a new *kind* of community. Gospel-centered churches are living proof that the good news is true, that Jesus is not a theory but is real, as he gives back to us our humanness. In its doctrine and culture, words and deeds, such a church makes visible the restored humanity only Christ can give.

In his powerful essay *2 Contents, 2 Realities*, Francis Schaeffer proposes four things that should mark a gospel-created church: sound doctrine, honest answers to honest questions, true spirituality, and the beauty of human relationships. Yet the last of those four, the beauty of human relationships, is the first thing that outsiders are likely to notice when they enter a church. True beauty makes people stop and stare. But "if we do not show beauty in the way we treat each other, then in the eyes of the world and in the eyes of our own children, we are destroying the truth we proclaim."[1]

A common objection to the gospel is this: "Look at your churches." No more needs to be said. A doubter can find a reason to disregard the truth claims of the gospel just by looking at the relational tone of our churches. And why not? It's in our churches that the gospel is field-tested for real life. If people want to know what the gospel creates, are they being unfair to look to a church? I don't think so.

Consider a parallel. If I want to examine Marxism, I can read two thousand tedious pages of *Das Kapital* by Karl Marx, or I can look at the countries that have put Marxism to work. The Soviet Union, for example, collapsed in 1991 under the weight of its own tragic stupidity. What went wrong? Did the Soviets fail to live by their Marxism? No, it was their faithfulness to Marxism that undid them. Marxism cannot work because it does not build on the truth about God and man. It builds on a fantasy of human self-idealization.

In a similar way, you can consider Christianity either by earning a PhD in biblical studies, or simply by getting up a little earlier next Sunday morning and visiting a church. The gospel should be displayed most clearly in our churches. Therefore, how we "behave in the household of God" matters to everyone around us.

This is the point Paul makes in 1 Timothy 3:14–16. Paul wanted to visit Timothy, but his travel plans were uncertain, so he mailed his thoughts on ahead. He says a number of great things in the letter—what the gospel is, what a leader is, what money is for, and so forth. But right in the middle Paul observes that he wrote the letter so "that [Timothy] may know how one ought to behave in the household of God, which is the church of the living God, a pillar and buttress of the truth" (1 Tim. 3:15).

COUNTERING ONE CULTURE WITH ANOTHER

Here is the insight embedded in these verses. The only answer to one culture is another culture—not just a concept, but a counterculture. A church should offer the world such a counterculture, a living embodiment of the gospel.

The culture we live in is "a pillar and buttress" for many false gospels. For instance, one of the destructive lies that informs Western culture today is what some call Moralistic Therapeutic Deism.[2] Here is its message:

1. A God exists and watches over human life on earth.
2. God wants people to be good, nice, and fair to each other.
3. The central goal of life is to be happy and to feel good about oneself.
4. God does not need to be particularly involved in one's life, except when he is needed to resolve a problem.
5. Good people go to heaven when they die.

What kind of culture does Moralistic Therapeutic Deism create? One in which we all do "whatever makes you feel good about you."[3] It hardly requires our repentance or displays God's power—and it offers no hope. Only judgment looms ahead. But this false religion is widespread today. Therefore, God calls our churches to stand out as a clear alternative to this bland but popular fraud.

There is nothing else like the church in the world today—a new kind of community created by God that makes the gospel visible and convincing in a world that believes everything *but* the gospel.

Jesus said, "I came to cast fire on the earth" (Luke 12:49). Elton Trueblood, in his book wonderfully entitled *The Incendiary Fellowship*, explains how that worked out in the early church:

> It was the incendiary character of the early Christian fellowship which was amazing to the contemporary Romans, and it was amazing precisely because there was nothing in their experience that was remotely similar to it. Religion they had in vast quantities, but it was nothing like this. . . . Much of the uniqueness of Christianity, in its original emergence, consisted of the fact that simple people could be amazingly powerful when they were members one of another. As everyone knows, it is almost impossible to create a fire with one log, even if it is a sound one, while several poor logs may make an excellent fire if they stay together as they burn. The miracle of the early church was that of poor sticks making a grand conflagration.[4]

When it comes to the church's witness, apologetics can contribute to the advance of the gospel. God graciously wants to satisfy the questions of our minds. So let's all improve at explaining the reasonableness of the gospel to our doubting friends. *But the beauty of human relationships in the church is itself an argument for the gospel*, just as a tender romance that endures for a lifetime is an argument for marriage when marriage is doubted. When the gospel is doubted, a beautiful church that sticks together is an unanswerable argument in our angry and divided world. Outsiders respond to it the way a young architect responded to L'Abri Fellowship in Switzerland: "I want to tell you," he said to Francis Schaeffer, "every time I have been here, I feel like a human being."[5] So he professed Christ.

Churches don't make the gospel true. It is true even when the household of God behaves badly. But people can *see* that it is true, and doubters are converted when "the sweetness of the Lord" is upon us (Ps. 90:17, JB).

So, realizing how strategic our churches are "in the defense and confirmation of the gospel" (Phil. 1:7), let's think through 1 Timothy 3:14–16.

THE HOUSEHOLD OF GOD

Paul's concern in this letter, as we have seen, is "how one ought to behave in the household of God" (1 Tim. 3:15).

The word *household* means a family. That's what a church is, because God is our Father (Eph. 2:18–19). He has adopted us as his children through Christ (Rom. 8:15). Justification clears us legally of guilt before our Judge, but adoption includes us emotionally in the heart of our Father. You might think of the difference between babysitting someone else's kids and watching your own. You sincerely care about the other kids, but you care differently about your own. To be graphic, when your child throws up on you, it is somehow not as disgusting as another child's, is it? That is how God loves us—as his own children, in all our mess.

But how should we behave in the household of God our Father?

Maybe when you were growing up, chaos reigned in your family. Maybe the kids and even the parents mouthed off and behaved cruelly. Some families are like that. Some churches are like that too.

But God's household must never be like that. Such behavior denies our Father. He wants us to behave in ways that reveal his heart and who he is. This means we must not import into our church families today the failed patterns of our earthly families in the past. We learn how to behave in the household of God not primarily by looking back at our families but by looking up at our Father: "Therefore be imitators of God, as beloved children" (Eph. 5:1). That's a new kind of community this world cannot create.

We see the Father most clearly in the Son. The likeness is so close that Jesus said, "Whoever has seen me has seen the Father" (John 14:9). How then can the broken world see the inexpressible beauty of the Father and Son in our churches? Few biblical passages say it better than Jesus's Beatitudes:

> Blessed are the poor in spirit, for theirs is the kingdom of heaven.
> Blessed are those who mourn, for they shall be comforted.
> Blessed are the meek, for they shall inherit the earth.
> Blessed are those who hunger and thirst for righteousness, for they shall be satisfied.
> Blessed are the merciful, for they shall receive mercy.

Blessed are the pure in heart, for they shall see God.
Blessed are the peacemakers, for they shall be called sons
of God.
Blessed are those who are persecuted for righteousness' sake,
for theirs is the kingdom of heaven. (Matt. 5:3–10)

The whole point of the Beatitudes is to tell us how to behave in the household of God. They set the tone of Jesus's new kingdom. It is striking that Jesus began his first extended sermon by emphasizing a gospel culture.

We might find it easier to see how big a change it is to enter into Christ's kingdom if we flip each of the Beatitudes to its opposite:

Blessed are the entitled, for they get their way.
Blessed are the carefree, for they are comfortable.
Blessed are the pushy, for they win.
Blessed are the self-righteous, for they need nothing.
Blessed are the vengeful, for they will be feared.
Blessed are those who don't get caught, for they look good.
Blessed are the argumentative, for they get in the last word.
Blessed are the winners, for they get their way.

Don't these "Beatitudes" describe this world? But which of these two cultures, the kingdom of Christ or the kingdom of this world, more accurately describes your church?

The household of God must offer a clear and lovely alternative to the madness of this world. In our churches, God calls us to reach for something better than what many of us have ever experienced.

The family of God is where people behave in a new way.

I think of it with a simple equation: gospel + safety + time. The family of God is where people should find lots of gospel, lots of safety, and lots of time. In other words, the people in our churches need:

- multiple exposures to the happy news of the gospel from one end of the Bible to the other;
- the safety of non-accusing sympathy so that they can admit their problems honestly; and
- enough time to rethink their lives at a deep level, because people are complex and changing is not easy.

In a gentle church like this, no one is put under pressure or singled out for embarrassment. Everyone is free to open up, and we all grow together as we look to Jesus. Behaving well in the household of God sets a tone defined by gospel + safety + time for everyone. This is what sets a church apart as a new kind of community.

John Calvin paints the picture of how God's forgiveness must continually wash over us in our churches to preserve and protect us:

Not only does the Lord through forgiveness of sins receive and adopt us once for all into the church, but through the same means he preserves and protects us there. For what would be the point of providing a pardon for us that was destined to be of no use? . . . So, carrying, as we do, the traces of sin around with us throughout life, unless we are sustained by the Lord's constant grace in forgiving our sins, we shall scarcely abide one moment in the church. But the Lord has called his children to eternal salvation. Therefore, they ought to ponder that there is pardon ever ready for their sins. Consequently, we must firmly believe that by God's generosity, mediated by Christ's merit, through the sanctification of the Spirit, sins have been and are daily pardoned to us who have been received and engrafted into the body of the church.[6]

Is that how sinners experience your church—as a safe place where the Lord "preserves and protects us"? Or do they experience your church as a place of shame and anxiety?

Church discipline is biblical, of course. It should occur when someone's misbehavior in the household of God desecrates the name of the Father and jeopardizes the safety of the other family members. The "deal-breaker" sin, which requires formal church discipline, is one that subverts the gospel culture itself—by gossip, for example.[7] As a pastor friend of mine recently said: "When a sinner is repentant, the elders should protect that sinner from the church. When a sinner is defiant, the elders should protect the church from that sinner."

The goal is not to make the church safe for sin; it's to make it safe for confession and repentance. When the gospel of Christ's grace defines both the doctrine and the culture of a church, its members can safely confess and forsake sin. Even "extreme" sinners find themselves wonderfully forgiven and freed.

THE CHURCH OF THE LIVING GOD

The assembled saints not only comprise the household of God, says Paul, they are "the church of the living God" (1 Tim. 3:15).

The word *church* means an assembly of people.[8] They are

not just a group or a demographic category. They are an actual *gathering* of people.

How could it be otherwise? We who believe in Jesus have been called out from what we were before. Now we thrive whenever we gather together in his name. Jesus said, "Come, for everything is now ready" (Luke 14:17). The Holy Spirit came down at Pentecost when "they were all together in one place" (Acts 2:1). His mighty power increased the church both in number and in depth of community (Acts 2:41–47). The church of Jerusalem in Acts loved getting together.

The gathered people of God are a powerful force for gospel-driven change. As some said in the radical days of the 1960s, "Revolution is seeing each other a lot."[9]

As the church "of the living God," we have been miraculously converted. Formerly, God was a prop on the stage of our self-centered dramas. We might have wanted him, but not too much of him. We wanted to be forgiven and to go to heaven, for sure. And we wanted him around when life became bad enough. But otherwise we preferred to be on our own. We were, in fact, allergic to God and alive to our own false ideals.

Then everything changed. The Holy Spirit awakened us to see God in a new way—not as our last resort but as our fountainhead. Down deep inside us now is a yearning for God that—though we remain inconsistent—keeps drawing us back to him as our most heartfelt desire. And that yearning will never die. We share that heartbeat together in our churches, and our Lord gives himself to us most potently in our gatherings, even the most humble ones: "Where two or three are gathered in my name, there am I among them" (Matt. 18:20).

That makes every faithful church a witness to the living God in a world of dead idols.

A PILLAR AND BUTTRESS OF THE TRUTH

Finally, Paul observes in this passage that the church is "a pillar and buttress of the truth" (1 Tim. 3:15). What does that mean? Well, what does a pillar do? It holds something up. And what does a buttress do? It firms something up. A faithful church, in other words, holds the gospel up for everyone to see and firms the gospel up as credible and solid.

Your church is called to be a pillar lifting high the truth of the gospel. The one truth that will outlast the universe, the one truth that can help sinners and sufferers right now, deserves to be put on clear display. We must not allow anything in our churches to compete with the high visibility of the gospel. A church has no right to act like a community bulletin board down at the local grocery store, covered over with business cards, ads for apartments for rent, notices about lost pets, and other agendas that compete for people's attention. A church exists to be a pillar that holds up the truth of Jesus so obviously that everyone can see it.

But a church is also called to be a buttress. Why? Because the gospel does not *feel* strong to many people. Other things grab their attention—a new diet plan, a better self-image, getting the kids into the right colleges. Such distractions feel like the key to a better future, while the gospel feels like an itty-bitty lifestyle option for the weekend among those with a religious bent. Many people make their decisions about the gospel based on how it *feels*. That's where the buttress comes in. A church can offer living and palpable proof that the gospel makes a real difference for real people living in the real world. That is also why we gather—to embody the truth of the gospel together so that people are intrigued by it. As a pillar and buttress of the truth, our churches are God's Plan A for world redemption, and he has no Plan B.

No church should exist to exalt itself, any more than a pillar or buttress should draw attention to itself. Every church exists for the glorious truth about Jesus Christ, who (Paul goes on to say in verse 16) "was manifested in the flesh, vindicated by the Spirit, seen by angels, proclaimed among the nations, believed on in the world, taken up in glory." Our churches are here for *him*, and him *only*. May every competing agenda fall down forever at his feet!

Every faithful church is dear to God's heart precisely because it displays Jesus in the fullness of his glory. Timothy Dwight (1752–1817), the president of Yale, felt this deeply, so he wrote:

> I love thy kingdom, Lord,
> the house of thine abode,
> the Church our blest Redeemer saved
> with his own precious blood.
>
> For her my tears shall fall,
> for her my prayers ascend,
> to her my cares and toils be given
> till toils and cares shall end.
>
> Beyond my highest joy
> I prize her heavenly ways,

her sweet communion, solemn vows,
her hymns of love and praise.[10]

Not many write strong lyrics like that today. Instead, people patch together their own versions of Christianity, pick and choose verses from the Bible, and sidestep costly church commitment. The problem with that is not just a low view of the church, it's a minimalist approach to Christianity. It is an attempt to get by with as little as possible and still "make the cut" as a Christian. It makes the Lord of glory look like a loser who is not worth living for. Where is *that* in the gospel?

The power of the gospel creates something altogether different in the world today. It creates churches that, to borrow from John Piper, are God-exalting, Christ-admiring, Spirit-filled, Bible-enjoying, grace-preaching, convenience-defying, cross-embracing, risk-taking, selfishness-crucifying, gossip-silencing, prayer-saturated, future-thinking, outward-reaching, and beautifully human congregations where the undeserving can thrive.[11] Only God can build this new kind of community. But when he does, it cannot be ignored.

Do you see the grandeur of your church, which is the household of God, the church of the living God, a pillar and buttress of the truth of the gospel? It is a new kind of community for the display of Christ's glory. "Out of Zion, the perfection of beauty, God shines forth" (Ps. 50:2).

5

IT ISN'T EASY,
BUT IT IS POSSIBLE

> But when I saw that their conduct was not in step with the truth of the gospel, I said to Cephas before them all, "If you, though a Jew, live like a Gentile and not like a Jew, how can you force the Gentiles to live like Jews?"
>
> Galatians 2:14

Believing the gospel is not easy. It says that an all-holy God loves sinners like us. It says he sent his only Son to die for us. It says that he pours out his Holy Spirit to give us life and to keep us. It claims that nothing will ever separate us from the love of God in Christ Jesus our Lord. It even says that this Savior is God's strategy to transform the universe. Does this good news not seem improbable? We either proudly believe that we are too good to be judged, or we proudly believe we are too bad to be saved. So the gospel is a continual surprise, and we need to hear it again and again.

One of the largest barriers to the work of the gospel in our churches is unbelief among us church members. Our unbelief impedes the gospel in ways we don't see, even as we intend to advance the gospel. Getting past our unbelief isn't easy, but it is possible. That's what we will consider in this chapter.

Martin Luther puts it plainly: "The gospel cannot be beaten into our ears enough or too much. Yes, though we learn it and understand it well, yet there is no one who takes hold of it perfectly or believes it with all his heart, so frail a thing is our flesh and disobedient to the Spirit."[1] It requires a new way of thinking to believe that God is for us *only* because of what Jesus earned. It means readjusting our perspective continually, to embrace the fact that our lives depend upon something from outside of us.

But God set it up this way long ago. In the garden of Eden, even before the complexities of sin entered the world, God arranged our existence so that we could thrive only when life is given to us from outside. He gave Adam and Eve the tree of life to constantly refresh them (Gen. 2:9, 16–17). In the same way, our vigor has never come from "in here" but always from "out there." We can receive life only with the empty hands of faith. God said to Adam, in effect:

> Listen, son, if you obey me, you will flourish. But if you disobey me, it will create in you a thing called "evil," which will lead to something called "death." You don't know what those things are, and you don't want to know. But if you will trust me, it will go well for you. All the richness and fullness of life will be yours.

Adam had to accept God's word and reach outward toward God for life moment by moment.

The temptation of the Devil was (and is): "Don't risk yourself on God. Trust your own instincts. Live from within yourself. You need to take control, because you cannot trust God." Adam fell for this temptation. As a result, we are now born bent in on ourselves. It feels normal to rest our hopes on ourselves. We create whole cultures to reinforce our idealized theories about ourselves.

The gospel changes us down deep at this intuitive level. When God justifies us in Christ, he directly counteracts our whole self-involved strategy for living. He credits a righteousness to us that depends on Someone Else, re-creating the Edenic relationship and drawing us out of ourselves into his fullness (John 1:16). We now live in Christ, the new and better Adam. At times, admittedly, our hearts still feel that we remain in a precarious position with God. We fear he will let us down. So we fall back into scurrying about to fill our emptiness with our own resources. But God graciously lets us wear ourselves out, and these efforts come to nothing. *Life exists not in us but in Christ alone and Christ fully. We live in him.*[2]

What's so surprising about this gospel is the exteriority, the out-there-ness, of all true life. But it's freeing. John Bunyan pictures that freedom in his own story:

> One day as I was passing in the field, and that too with some dashes on my conscience, fearing lest all was still not right, suddenly this sentence fell upon my soul, *Your righteousness is in heaven*. And I thought as well that I saw, with the eyes of my soul, Jesus Christ at God's right hand. There, I say, is my righteousness, so that wherever I was or whatever I was doing, God could not say of me, *He lacks my righteousness*, for that was just before Him. I also saw that it was not my good frame of heart that made my righteousness better, nor my bad frame that made

my righteousness worse, for my righteousness was Jesus Christ Himself, the same yesterday and today and forever. Now did my chains fall off my legs indeed. . . . Now I went home rejoicing for the grace and love of God. . . . Here I lived for some time, very sweetly at peace with God through Christ. Oh, I thought, Christ! Christ! There was nothing but Christ before my eyes.[3]

That's what gospel doctrine is *for*—to show weak and unworthy people like us a picture of Christ in his grace and glory. We lose sight of him quickly, don't we? We all need frequent exposures to his overruling good news.

THE DIFFICULTY OF CULTIVATING A GOSPEL CULTURE

A gospel culture is harder to lay hold of than gospel doctrine. It requires more relational wisdom and finesse. It involves stepping into a kind of community unlike anything we've experienced, where we happily live together on a love we can't create. A gospel culture requires us not to bank on our own importance or virtues, but to forsake self-assurance and exult together in Christ alone.

This mental adjustment is not easy, but living in this kind of community is wonderful. We find ourselves saying with Paul, "For his sake I have suffered the loss of all things"—all the trophies of our self-importance, all the wounds of our self-pity, every self-invented thing that we lug around as a way of getting attention—"and count them as [dung,[4]] in order that I may gain Christ and be found in him, not having a righteousness of my own that comes from the law, but that which comes through faith in Christ" (Phil. 3:8–9). Paul did not regard the loss of his inflated self as sacrificial. Who admires his own dung? It is a relief to be rid of our distasteful egos! And when a whole church together luxuriates in Christ alone, that church embodies a gospel culture. It becomes a surprising new kind of community where sinners and sufferers come alive because the Lord is there, giving himself freely to the desperate and undeserving.

But how easy it is for a church to exist in order to puff itself up! How hard it is to forsake our own glory for a higher glory!

The primary barrier to displaying the beauty of Jesus in our churches comes from the way we re-insert ourselves into that sacred center that belongs to him alone. Exalting ourselves always diminishes his visibility. That is why cultivating a gospel culture requires a profound, moment by moment "unselfing" by every one of us. It is personally costly, even painful. What I am proposing throughout this book is not glib or shallow. So much is set against us, within and without. But the triumph of the gospel in our churches is still possible, as we look to Christ alone. He will help us.

We need God's wisdom to build a gospel culture because every culture consists not just of what we see but also what we see *with*—even our unexamined assumptions. We don't naturally notice our church's culture, the way a fish doesn't notice water, but culture is a powerful reality. It shapes our identity, values, and sense of possibilities. It subtly defines the terms for feeling okay about ourselves—that we belong and that we matter.

EVALUATING OUR CHURCH CULTURES

Therefore, we should not assume that our church culture is true to Christ in every way. We should assume that it isn't, and in ways we haven't yet noticed. We should pay careful attention to the intangibles of our churches—the feel, ethos, relationships, quality, and unspoken assumptions. They might not be in alignment with the gospel as closely as we desire.

To discern more clearly the culture of your church, ask yourself several questions. What is the most important thing about your church that has never been formally decided upon? Is there some well-intentioned but unhelpful ideal? Is there some place in your church's life where obedience to Christ is being withheld but his blessing is expected anyway? Is there something that has too strong a grip on your church? It is easy for churches to make sacred cows of things, from handbell choirs to youth programs to missions strategies. All of these can be good things, but they must always be surrendered to Christ.

By answering such questions, you might find two things: first, an idol, where your church claims too much for itself and thereby hinders your freedom in Christ; and, second, the very place where your church can learn more of the all-sufficiency of Jesus.

Life is in Christ, and in him alone. Every church can have more of his power by pressing the gospel more fully into its culture. It's no disaster for a church to suddenly find itself having to depend radically on Jesus. Dependence on him is a sign of health. Charles Haddon Spurgeon wisely says:

> It seems to me that the most Scriptural system of church government is that which requires the most prayer, the most faith, and the most piety to keep it going. The church of God was never

meant to be an automaton. If it were, the wheels would all act of themselves. The church was meant to be a *living* thing, a living person, and as the person cannot be supported if life is absent, or if food is kept back, or if breath is suspended, so should it be with the church.[5]

There will be times in a church's life when we feel that everything is falling apart. But such times can crack open a church's heart to depend on the living Christ as never before. They teach us that the best way to "do church" is always to place our endless need before his endless supply, as Spurgeon said. A. W. Tozer states the alternatives starkly:

Pseudo-faith always arranges a way out to serve in case God fails it. Real faith knows only one way and gladly allows itself to be stripped of any second way or makeshift substitutes. For true faith, it is either God or total collapse. And not since Adam first stood up on the earth has God failed a single man or woman [or church] who trusted Him.[6]

It is hard for us to trust the Lord so daringly. The false safety of self is an enduring problem for us Christians.

THE POWER OF FEAR IN A CHURCH'S CULTURE

The desire for false safety was a problem even among the apostles. This is one of the lessons we learn from the famous confrontation between Paul and Peter, which Paul recounts in his letter to the Galatians:

When Cephas came to Antioch, I opposed him to his face, because he stood condemned. For before certain men came from

> James, he was eating with the Gentiles; but when they came he drew back and separated himself, fearing the circumcision party. And the rest of the Jews acted hypocritically along with him, so that even Barnabas was led astray by their hypocrisy. (2:11–13)

John Stott calls this "one of the most tense and dramatic episodes in the New Testament."[7] It was not a case of personal rivalry. It was a clash between the gospel and tradition. Paul could see that nothing less than the gospel was at stake. He refused to stand by in silence while other leaders destroyed a gospel culture for the sake of an obsolete tradition that left self undisturbed.

There was nothing intrinsically wrong with Peter's Jewish customs. But there was something very wrong with requiring adherence to them after Christ had fulfilled them, which Peter did by distancing himself from the unkosher Gentile believers. In effect, Peter was saying that Gentiles had to believe the gospel *and* adapt to Jewish culture for them to be good enough for Christ—and good enough for Peter! They were not his equals, because they weren't like him. In doing this, Peter obscured the all-sufficiency of Jesus and exalted something of himself in the Lord's place. What an insult to the finished work of Christ on the cross! How demeaning to those blood-bought Gentiles! What an arrogant exaggeration of Peter's tradition! What a violation of justification by faith alone! And what a pathetic church culture!

The clean/unclean laws had long been observed by the Jews, rooted as they were in the Old Testament. The *Mishnah* (the Jewish applications of the Old Testament) even said that "the dwelling-places of Gentiles are unclean."[8] Peter had been careful all his life not to catch the Gentile contagion. But then God showed him that Jesus had fulfilled the old rules. Three times God taught Peter, "What God has made clean, do not call common" (Acts 10:15–16). The point couldn't be missed.

What drove Peter here in Antioch was not ignorance but fear of human disapproval: "He drew back and separated himself, *fearing the circumcision party.*" Like all of us, Peter had a history of fear. When he denied Jesus on the night of his Lord's arrest, he feared physical harm. In Antioch, he effectively denied Jesus because he feared social harm. Driven by that primitive fear, he falsified the gospel.

In other words, the problem entered in not at the level of doctrine but at the level of culture. It started with personal fear, not with reading a book of bad theology. So Paul twice called it hypocrisy: "And the rest of the Jews acted *hypocritically* along with him, so that even Barnabas was led astray by their *hypocrisy.*" Peter's example pressured Gentile believers to conform outwardly to Jewish customs, in order to be fully accepted members of the church.

Fear of human disapproval feeds political posturing. It makes us want to be perceived in a certain way and identified with certain people. It destroys honesty, spontaneity, and joy. It builds walls that Jesus died to tear down. It corrupts good doctrine, as we'll consider just below. And what is this fear but empty and unfulfilled selves being driven by something other than Jesus?

Sadly, fear can be a powerful force among Christians. Peter's fear was so influential that even Barnabas, the "son of encouragement" (Acts 4:36), was swept away. Paul alone had the clarity and courage to demand that the apostles reapply the original doctrine to their culture, so that the gospel message would go forward unhindered.

RIGHT DOCTRINE + WRONG CULTURE = DOCTRINAL DENIAL

In response to Peter's hypocrisy, Paul took a bold stand "so that the truth of the gospel might be preserved for you" (Gal. 2:5). He was not interested in the mere recitation of the gospel but in a clear understanding of it. Why? Paul knew that it is possible for us to unsay by our practical church culture what we say in our official church doctrine. It is possible to hold to the gospel as a theory even as we lose it as a reality. Let us express this insight simply and boldly:

Right gospel doctrine + anti-gospel culture =
a denial of the gospel

We might not notice that this is happening in our church if we look only at our statement of faith and tell ourselves, "We believe the right things." So it was with Peter. Paul recounts what he said to Peter: "We also have believed in Christ Jesus, in order to be justified by faith" (v. 16). It appears that this "we" includes Peter. So Peter never denied true gospel doctrine. But he contradicted the true gospel's culture of acceptance through his *behavior*, as Paul shows in verses 15 to 21. Peter was effectively rebuilding the culture of self-salvation he himself had torn down by his faith in Christ: "For if I rebuild what I tore down, I prove myself to be a transgressor" (v. 18).

But Paul refused to "nullify the grace of God" (v. 21), a claim that reveals what's really at stake. We can sincerely love the doctrine of God's grace and, at the same time, unwittingly nullify that grace. Preserving the truth requires a culture where sinners can see the beauty of what we believe in a new kind of community.

Building such a culture is not easy, but it is possible. The hard step for a church is confronting itself, even as Paul confronted Peter:

> But when I saw that their conduct was not in step with the truth of the gospel, I said to Cephas before them all, "If you, though a Jew, live like a Gentile and not like a Jew, how can you force the Gentiles to live like Jews?" (v. 14)

It's not enough for us to ask, does our church teach gospel doctrine? We must also ask, is our church culture clearly aligned with that gospel doctrine? For Paul, faithfulness to the gospel includes *applying* the gospel to our conduct: "I saw that *their conduct* was *not in step* with the truth of the gospel . . ." (v. 14a). The gospel gives us more than a place to stand; it also leads us into a path to follow. There is a way to live "in step" with it. It is a journey into more and more of the endless all-sufficiency of the Lord Jesus Christ. When our churches are open to all that Christ is for us, the gospel message becomes unmistakable and the way to Christ obviously open to all alike.

Galatians 2:11–14 is clear. All who trust Jesus for their justification are clean before God, whatever their background. If God declares us kosher through Christ alone, no one can rightly demand more. That is the gospel doctrine. That doctrine then creates a culture of gracious acceptance for all kinds of believers. Jesus said, "My yoke is easy" (Matt. 11:30). He takes it easy on people. He never forces people to playact what God has not required. But people passionately committed to gospel doctrine can create a tough church culture, as Peter did.

Gospel culture is just as sacred as gospel doctrine, and it must be carefully nurtured and preserved in our churches. Paul fought for it, because the doctrine of salvation by grace cannot be preserved with integrity if it is surrounded by a culture of salvation by self. Jesus is all the Savior anyone will ever need. He is our Tree of Life. He is enough to keep us alive forever, and he is freely available to everyone on the same basis.

THE WONDERFUL LIBERATION OF A GOSPEL CULTURE

How wonderful it is to come every Sunday into a liberating church! All week long we swim in an ocean of judgment and negative scrutiny. We constantly have to comply with the demands of a touchy world, and we never measure up. Swiss psychiatrist Paul Tournier characterizes "normal" human interactions as a cycle of criticism, guilt, and self-justification:

> In everyday life we are continually soaked in this unhealthy atmosphere of mutual criticism, so much so that we are not always aware of it and we find ourselves drawn unwittingly into an implacable vicious circle: every reproach evokes a feeling of guilt in the critic as much as in the one criticized, and each one gains relief from his guilt in any way he can, by criticizing other people and in self-justification.[9]

Then, on Sunday, we walk into a new kind of community where we discover an environment of grace in Christ alone. It is so refreshing. Sinners like us can breathe again! It's as if God simply changes everyone's topic of conversation from what's wrong with us, which is plenty, to what's right with Christ, which is endless. He replaces our negativity, finger-pointing, and self-hatred with the good news of his grace for the undeserving. Who couldn't come alive in a community that's constantly inhaling that heavenly atmosphere?

Here is where every one of us can happily take a stand right now: "The life I now live in the flesh I live by faith in the Son of God, who loved me and gave himself for me" (Gal. 2:20). Our self-focus was crucified with Christ. The need to conceal failure and display false superiority no longer lives. Christ is enough to complete every one of us, without adding anything of ourselves.

As we humbly keep in step with the truth of this gospel, people will find a new kind of community in our churches where sinners and sufferers can thrive. If confrontation is ever needed, it is only "so that the truth of the gospel might be preserved for you" (v. 5).

LOOKING TO HIM ALONE

A gospel culture is not easy. But it is possible. There is nothing mechanical or formulaic about living by faith in Christ. It means looking away from ourselves to him. It means deep self-surrender moment by moment. It means frequent mid-course corrections as our hearts and our churches get back into alignment with the Son of God, who loved us and gave himself for us.

As we look to him, he will help us. Martin Luther points us to where our new life will be found:

> Think carefully who this Son of God is, how glorious he is, how mighty he is. What is heaven and earth in comparison with him? . . . The law did not love me or give itself for me. Indeed, it accuses me, terrifies me, and drives me to despair. But now I have someone who has set me free from the terrors of the law, sin, and death, and has brought me to freedom, the righteousness of God, and eternal life. He is the Son of God, to whom be praise and glory forever. . . . Read these words, "he loved me and gave himself for me," with great emphasis. With a firm faith you may engrave this "me" on your heart and apply it to yourself, not doubting that you are among those to whom this "me" belongs.[10]

6

WHAT WE CAN EXPECT

> We are the aroma of Christ to God among those
> who are being saved and among those who are
> perishing, to one a fragrance from death to
> death, to the other a fragrance from life to life.
> Who is sufficient for these things?
>
> 2 Corinthians 2:15–16

As our churches press further into gospel doctrine and gospel culture, what can we expect to see? The Lord has different plans for different churches. But the Bible encourages us to look for more conversions (Acts 6:7), more joy (Acts 8:8), more impact (Acts 19:20), more glorious outcomes. We can also expect more trouble.

God spreads the fragrance of the knowledge of Christ as we preach the gospel of divine mercy and clothe that message in the beauty of a mercy-sharing corporate life (2 Cor. 2:14). We might expect, therefore, that the world would roll out the red carpet for us. But the Bible tells us to expect two opposite reactions simultaneously. Some people will experience our churches as "a fragrance from life to life." Others will experience them as "a fragrance from death to death." The more compelling our churches become through the gospel, the more intense these two reactions will be. We can expect both more openness and more controversy. Going forward with the Lord means that the future will be both more thrilling and more stressful than the present.

This is what Paul discovered as he travelled the Mediterranean world, spreading the gospel and planting churches. One man with one message produced two opposite outcomes. Why? Because it wasn't about Paul. It was about Christ in Paul. Our Lord was destined to trigger strong responses—for and against (Luke 2:34). He always did and he always will, until he returns.

When we find that our ministries both please and provoke, we should not be surprised. Nothing is going wrong. Rather, something is going right. God is spreading the fragrance of Christ through us.

Paul wrote 2 Corinthians 2:15–16 to explain this and to encourage us to keep steadily on course, surrendering to God's surprising strategy of judgment and salvation. That's the topic of this chapter.

WE ARE THE AROMA OF CHRIST

Paul writes, "We are the aroma of Christ to God among those who are being saved and among those who are perishing" (2 Cor. 2:15). The emphatic words are *of Christ*. It is the strong scent *of Christ* that people detect when our churches are filled with the gospel. How amazing that they should experience Christ himself through us! We are so unlike him in so many ways. Still, his scent comes through.

Even more wonderfully, we are "a Christ-like fragrance rising up *to God*" (NLT). That is Paul's main point here. Whatever people might think of us, God savors us as we lift up Jesus Christ crucified. One commentator writes, "Nothing delights the heart of God more than the preaching of the gospel of Christ."[1]

In what sense are we an "aroma"? The imagery comes from the Old Testament. It's used as early as the episode of Noah's sacrifice—"the LORD smelled the pleasing aroma" (Gen. 8:21)—and it shows up in the laws about sacrifices in Leviticus (e.g. Lev. 1:9, 13, 17, etc.). It pleased God that Noah and the Levitical priests offered atoning sacrifices, bearing witness to God's merciful way with sinners. Likewise, it pleased God that Christ offered the ultimate atonement in himself at the cross. And it pleases God today when we offer ourselves and our churches as living sacrifices (Rom. 12:1) for the display of the gospel of Christ. Throughout the Bible, God's pleasure comes to a focal point at the cross of Christ. This sacrifice was foreshadowed in Old Testament times; it was actualized in Christ himself; and it's reenacted in us today.

It has been said, "It is the *burning* of the offering that makes it a pleasing aroma."[2] And churches where hearts burn with the gospel give off the aroma of Christ himself, wonderful to God in heaven above. There is much about us that God graciously overlooks. What he notices, and what pleases him, is our churches' passion for Christ crucified.

But down here on earth, among people, it's often a different story. People's opinions of us gravitate toward two opposite extremes. And the clearer our churches are about Christ, the more polarizing we will be.

"Among those who are being saved," we are a sweet fragrance of Christ himself. People are cheered and helped by our gospel, as if the Lord himself were present in our efforts, because his Spirit is. These people enter in and join us.

"Among those who are perishing," we give off an offensive stink. People wonder what's wrong with us, why we don't get it, why we don't bathe in a shower of up-to-date thought. These people turn up their noses. Yet even when people are offended, our gospel ministries remain sweet to God above.

What insight do we gain from these two strong reactions? What is the Bible saying that can help us amid the bewildering complexity of human opinions, positive and negative? It's what John Calvin said so simply about the gospel: "It is never preached in vain."[3]

Jesus's purpose in coming into the world was not condemnation but salvation (John 3:17). Yet to this day, some people show an allergic reaction to his saving gospel. They break out in a rash of rejection, even while other people get healthier and healthier. Notice the present tenses in 2 Corinthians 2:15: "*are* being saved" and "*are* perishing." Some people are on the road to eternal ruin. The gospel whispers to them: "Everything you most deeply believe in is destroying you even now. You are completely wrong. Run to Christ!" But they don't. Others are on the road to eternal life. The gospel declares to them: "Everything you most deeply hope for is becoming real in you even now. Stick with Christ!" And they do. The gospel makes a felt impact on both kinds of people.

But the one thing the gospel never does is nothing.

The gospel of the Lord Jesus Christ refuses to be held at arm's length with critical detachment. No one judges the gospel. It judges all, and it saves some.

We must take this to heart ourselves. Every time we hear the gospel preached, it hardens us a little more, or it softens us a little more, depending on our heart's condition before God. We cannot stay safely the same, as if we were in control. Martyn Lloyd-Jones counsels us wisely:

> Be careful how you treat God, my friends. You may say to yourself, "I can sin against God and then, of course, I can repent and go back and find God whenever I want him." You try it. And you will sometimes find that not only can you not find God but that you do not even want to. You will be aware of a terrible hardness in your heart. And you can do nothing about it. And then you suddenly realize that it is God punishing you in order to reveal your sinfulness and your vileness to you. And there is only one thing to do. You turn back to him and you say, "O God, do not go on dealing with me judicially, though I deserve it. Soften my heart. Melt me. I cannot do it myself." You cast yourself utterly upon his mercy and upon his compassion.[4]

We sinners do not manage the power of God. We only prove his power, one way or the other, and reveal the truth about ourselves.

FROM DEATH TO DEATH, FROM LIFE TO LIFE

In fact, exposure to the gospel makes the true condition of people's hearts more and more obvious, as Paul explains further. Our gospel aroma is "to one a fragrance from death to death, to the other a fragrance from life to life" (2 Cor. 2:16). Not only do people's responses to gospel-saturated churches reveal their hearts toward Christ himself, their responses also move them further and further along. "From death to death" means they are falling still deeper into death, driven by revulsion at the stench of the gospel. They are spiraling downward from bad to worse in a condition irreversible apart from God's intervening mercy. "From life to life" means their born-again hearts are growing more alive, more sincere, more sensitive, drawn on and on by the sweet fragrance of Christ in the same gospel.

But no one is static. No one is *not* responding to the gospel. Everyone is moving further along one path or the other.

Naturally, we want to remove from our churches every obstacle to accepting Christ and growing in him (Isa. 57:14–15; 2 Cor. 6:3). We want to adapt our communication wisely and humbly (1 Cor. 9:19–23; 10:32–11:1). We want to satisfy people's doubts and difficulties as much as we can (Col. 4:5–6; 1 Pet. 3:15). But we can never make a negative response impossible as we effectively communicate the gospel. An angry, cynical, fault-finding, from-death-to-death rejection is not our failure. Rejection is built into gospel ministry because of the nature of the fallen human heart.

I hasten to add, of course, how ugly it would be to gloat over someone in that horrible condition! We must weep over people for whom no gospel presentation is ever good enough, people who are not satisfied because they are not satisfiable. They are moving away from Jesus and toward death. But we must never be deflected from faithfulness to Christ because of human rejection. Something profound is happening, deeper than any adjustments we can make in our gospel presentation.

Still, it is *through us* that God spreads the fragrance of the knowledge of Christ (2 Cor. 2:14). That is staggering. Through our ministries, people's eternal destinies are appearing even now in time. And their rejection of our gospel ministry is sobering to us. It would be better for them never to have heard it at all. No wonder Paul says, "Who is sufficient for these things?" The gospel is sufficient for all of God's purposes, of course. But we are not sufficient. We do our best week after week, but we are small and inadequate.

The deeper reality is that we are being caught up in God's own work of salvation and judgment. Eternal consequences hang in the balance in every gathering of the church, every Bible study, every personal conversation, every blog post. Heaven and hell are beginning to appear in people before our very eyes. And that we would say something that proves fatal to one and saving to another—who is equal to such a role?

The ministry of the gospel in our churches involves more than doctrinal argumentation. The work of the gospel is subtle, like the work of a fragrance. It is not just brute facts landing hard on someone's mind, but an aroma wafting into a heart. And this light contact proves to be life or death. Such is the astonishing power of the gospel of God.

MISDIRECTED BLAME

As Christians, we should not be discouraged when we are misjudged and mistreated. It is part of gospel ministry. We should expect it and accept it for the Lord's sake. Those who refuse the Christ that we proclaim rarely admit that their choice is against him. To justify themselves, they look for ways to blame us. Yes, we should always admit our true failings with utter honesty. But it is striking how confident the apostles were, how absent from the New Testament is a spirit of self-accusation. Hand-wringing appears nowhere in 2 Corinthians 2:15–16, where Paul sums up his whole ministry.

One way to neutralize the impact of a faithful church is to allow a spirit of improper self-doubt. Charles Haddon Spurgeon says: "Oh, 'tis terribly and solemnly true, that of all sinners some sanctuary sinners are the worst. Those who can dive deepest into sin, and have the most quiet consciences and hardest hearts, are some who are to be found in God's own house."[5] When such people stir up controversy within a church, some well-meaning person often complicates the difficulty by saying, "But in every conflict, there is always wrong on both sides." Really? In many conflicts, yes. But in *every* conflict? That is not what the Bible says.

The first "church split" in the Bible was pretty one-sided—Cain murdered his brother Abel over a controversy regarding worship (Gen. 4:1–12). And what was so wrong with Abel that Cain felt justified in destroying his brother? The Bible answers:

> We should not be like Cain, who was of the evil one and murdered his brother. And why did he murder him? Because his own deeds were evil and his brother's righteous. Do not be surprised, brothers, that the world hates you. (1 John 3:12–13)

Both Cain and Abel were sinners. But what triggered the conflict was that Cain's deeds were evil and his brother's were righteous, and Cain couldn't stand it.

When any church has worldly members whose hearts are not yet new, this scenario replays over and over until that worldliness is confronted and gospel sincerity is restored. For instance, people might accuse faithful gospel ministries of being unloving, which is an easy charge to make but nearly impossible to prove or disprove. We who lead must discern what is really going on by applying biblical categories of assessment. John Piper makes this vividly concrete:

> I have seen so much emotional blackmail in my ministry, I am jealous to raise a warning against it. Emotional blackmail happens when a person equates his or her emotional pain with another person's failure to love. They aren't the same. A person may love well and the beloved still feel hurt, and use the hurt to blackmail the lover into admitting guilt he or she does not have. Emotional blackmail says, "If I feel hurt by you, you are guilty." There is no defense. The hurt person has become God. His emotion has become judge and jury. Truth does not matter. All that matters is the sovereign suffering of the aggrieved. It is above question. This emotional device is a great evil. I have seen it often in my three decades of ministry and I am eager to defend people who are being wrongly indicted by it.[6]

In an age when personal unhappiness is often regarded as someone else's fault, some people walk into church looking for a scapegoat. The leaders of the church are easy prey. The people's angry perception of those leaders is, as Dr. Piper suggests, logically confused but psychologically compelling within their own thought world, and they readily spread that perception to other people. Then, in the name of "reconciliation," those leaders might feel pressure to confess as sin aspects of their ministry that are, in fact, true to the gospel and loving to the people.

ENEMIES AND A FRIEND

Again, let's stay humble and honestly admit every failing. But 2 Corinthians 2:15–16 teaches us that the opposition we face can well indicate how faithful we are to our provocative Lord's provocative gospel.

Faithfulness makes enemies on earth. But faithfulness also has a Friend and Advocate on high:

> Blessed are you when others revile you and persecute you and utter all kinds of evil against you falsely on my account. Rejoice and be glad, for your reward is great in heaven, for so they persecuted the prophets who were before you. (Matt. 5:11–12)

7

OUR PATH FORWARD

They follow the Lamb wherever he goes.

Revelation 14:4 (NIV)

In all this world, there is:

> no truth so solid as gospel doctrine,
> no community so humane as a gospel culture,
> nothing so resisted and yet so redemptive as both together, and
> nothing so worthy of our utmost devotion.

I hope you are convinced that gospel doctrine is true to the Bible and that gospel culture is humanizing to people. If so, what's next? What's required of us? What will it take for the gospel, which we love, to renew the churches we also love?

Given the corruption of our hearts (Jer. 17:9), the first thing to do is to kneel before God and humbly beg him to hold on to us. Every one of us is always five minutes away from moral and ministry disaster. Let's be realistic about how contrary our desires can be to the ways of God. You and I are not the saviors. There is only one Savior. Therefore, we must hurl ourselves into his arms right now, and never stop doing so, moment by moment, as long as we live. Francis Schaeffer used to say: "We are not building God's kingdom. He is building his kingdom, and we are praying for the privilege of being involved."

Within the range of the opportunities he graciously gives, I see three simple treasures that every one of us and our churches can reach for: power, courage, and love. I see no advance without them. They are biblical. They require no money or particular worship style. They can work in any church of any denomination as long as the gospel itself—and the gospel alone—is allowed to stand at the defining center of that church.

If we have suffered the loss of all things in order to gain Christ—no egos to protect or scores to settle—we are free to receive his power, courage, and love. They outperform everything in this world, because they come from beyond this world. How compelling for our churches to say: "We're not taking one more step without the power, courage, and love of the gospel for the glory of Christ alone. No more status quo!"

Let's think about each of these three treasures.

POWER

First is power. The gospel is the power of God (Rom. 1:16), and Jesus said his followers would be "clothed with power from on high" (Luke 24:49). On the day of Pentecost, sure enough, "suddenly there came from heaven a sound like a mighty rushing wind" (Acts 2:2). That power didn't come from the pastor, the people, or the praise band. It came from heaven, suddenly, without explanation except that God was in it.

How can we take up the name of Christ without the power of Christ? If our purposes rise no higher than what we can attain by our own organizing and thinking, then we should change our churches into community centers. But if we are weary of ourselves and our own brilliance, if we are embarrassed by our failures, then we are ready for the gift of power from on high.

Too often we regard God's power as an added ingredient that turbocharges our own efforts. The early church didn't think that way. They thought of God's power as a miraculous intervention without which they were dead in the water. Not even gospel words were expected to work in an automatic way. The apostle Paul defined authentic ministry among the Thessalonians like this: "Our gospel came to you not only in word, but also in power and in the Holy Spirit and with full conviction" (1 Thess. 1:5). The coming of the gospel provoked an encounter, a clash between the claims of Thessalonian culture and the claims of an eternal kingdom. It turned the Thessalonians from their self-invented idols to serve the living and true God (1 Thess. 1:9). The idea that God might enhance their powers merely by adding his power was the furthest thing from the minds of these believers.

How can we press more deeply into the power of God today? The answer will always be simple. All we can do is go back to our Lord and his grace: "Be strengthened by the grace that is in Christ Jesus" (2 Tim. 2:1).

Does that answer seem too easy, even a letdown? Then try it. It is never easy. It means deliberately rejecting every other source of strength but the grace of Christ alone. Such rejection is counterintuitive to self-assured, get-it-done, pragmatic Christians like us. Our cleverness always seems to promise more impact. But that cleverness, in fact, is a liability brilliantly disguised as an asset. The real battle being fought in our times is so profound it can be won only by the grace that is in Christ Jesus alone. All other weapons of war lead to flight, defeat, and disgrace. But strengthened by his grace, we will stumble forward into victory after victory.

Since we are thinking here about power from God, you might expect me to call for more prayer. Yes, let's pray more! We will never experience God without depending on God and calling on God. Pastor Eric Alexander of the Church of Scotland explains how prayer really factors into our work: "Prayer is *the essence* of the work to which God calls us. We frequently speak about praying *for* the work, but essentially it is prayer which *is* the real work."[1]

It is rare today to see a passion for prayer as the essence of gospel ministry. But I also believe it is futile to try to work people up into prayer. It just doesn't get results beyond a surge of enthusiasm that soon wears off. I know of only one infallible way to get a church praying, and to keep it praying, for the power of God to come down: we need to fail. We need to fail so badly and obviously that we find out how much we really do trust ourselves rather than God. We need to be shocked by the collapse of our best methods. But what a blessing catastrophic disaster is, with all its misery and shame, if it turns us back to God!

Even the apostle Paul learned the hard way. God gave him a vision of heaven (2 Cor. 12:1–4). But that sacred experience did not secure his breakthrough to power. Instead it was his "thorn in the flesh," the pain that reduced him to distressing weakness (vv. 5–10). It was there in his desperate need that the Lord met him powerfully. Then his ministry got traction as never before. "That is why, for Christ's sake, I delight in weaknesses, in insults, in hardships, in persecutions, in difficulties. For when I am weak, then I am strong" (v. 10, NIV).

Here then are the choices we all face moment by moment: Will we aim to be impressive? Will we expect to be in complete control? Will we ensure that we always come out on top as winners? Or will we be happy for the power of Christ to rest upon us in our endless weakness? "No man can give at once the impressions that he himself is clever and that Jesus Christ is mighty to save."[2] Neither can any church.

COURAGE

The second treasure is courage. Jesus said, "Whoever would save his life will lose it, but whoever loses his life for my sake and the gospel's will save it" (Mark 8:35).

There is only one way to serve our Lord—in total dedication, whatever the cost, "that in everything he might be preeminent" (Col. 1:18). Henry Drummond used to say: "Don't touch Christianity unless you are willing to seek the Kingdom of Heaven first. I promise you a miserable existence if you seek it second."[3]

The gospel never advances without someone paying a price. It takes courage to live in the reality of that cost, but it is also freeing. We are no longer encumbered with self-interest, no longer imprisoned within past accomplishments, no longer intimidated by past failures. Instead, we are free to run the race set before us, looking to Jesus alone.

Therefore, we must relocate ourselves mentally at the starting line of that race we're going to run, at the foot of the mountain we're going to climb, and rejoice over it as life's greatest adventure—and do the next hard thing.

The greatness of Christ creates courage in us. Paul writes, "Forgetting what lies behind and straining forward to what lies ahead, I press on" (Phil. 3:13–14). That is how *mature* Christians think (v. 15). They are gripped by the gospel, and become eager, open, and forward-looking.

A mature pastor does not treat his church as a reckless roll of the dice, but he is sincerely open to a searching and substantive reformation of that church. Every pastor is wise to ask, "What is there in our church that is worth protecting at all costs?" Some things are, but not everything is.

If you are a church leader and you have settled down in your ministry, grinding out a boring routine and picking up a regular paycheck and holding on until retirement, your problem is not a lack of opportunity. Your problem is that you've lost sight of the glory of Jesus. You've settled for something less. You need to repent of every inferior glory and serve your Lord again with joyful abandon.

If you feel little restlessness for new blessing on your church, maybe you have forgotten whose church it is. It is not your own. It was bought with a price, and it belongs to Another. Let him have his way, according to his Word alone, for his glory alone. Trust him that, with every false treasure you surrender, he will more than bless you with true spiritual riches.

The primary barrier to the ministry of the gospel through your church is not out in the world; the primary barrier is within your church itself. Every church, to some extent, clogs and hinders the gospel, even as we intend to advance the gospel. So each one of our churches should examine itself. Then we should make every adjustment, however painful, however embarrassing, however controversial, out of love for the Lord Jesus Christ. He will honor our courage, because it springs from faith.

Scripture shows us the early church valuing boldness above life itself (Acts 4:23–31). How thrilling it is for our churches today to put the Lord first, confident that he has gospel purposes for us. It is joyous for a church to stand together as one and say: "We don't know exactly how this is going to play out. But we're going to trust the Lord and move forward, because all that matters to us is the greater glory of Jesus in our world today."

New courage always begins with the leaders. Whatever the leaders are, their entire church will eventually become. If the leaders are about business only, even the church's worship will become businesslike. But if the leaders are courageous for Christ, their church will be too. John Heuss, an Episcopal pastor of a previous generation, speaks to us today:

> It is a growing conviction of mine that no parish can fulfill its true function unless there is at the very center of its leadership life a small community of quietly fanatic, changed and truly converted Christians. The trouble with most parishes is that nobody, including the pastor, is really greatly changed. But even when there is a devoted self-sacrificing minister at the heart of the fellowship, not much will happen until there is a community of changed men and women. . . . We do not want ordinary

men. Ordinary men cannot win the brutally pagan life of a city like New York for Christ. We want quiet fanatics.[4]

It's not just an Episcopalian. Howard Guinness, an early leader in InterVarsity Christian Fellowship, challenges us similarly:

> Where are the men who say "no" to self, who take up Christ's cross to bear it after him, . . . who are willing, if need be, to bleed, to suffer and to die on it? . . . Where are the adventurers, the explorers, the buccaneers for God, who count one human soul of far greater value than the rise or fall of an empire? . . . Where are the men who are willing to pay the price of vision? . . . Where are God's men in this day of God's power?[5]

Finally, no one less than Jonathan Edwards counsels all of us:

> Two things urgently needed in ministers, if they would attempt great advances for the kingdom of Christ, are zeal and resolve. Their influence and power for impact are greater than we think. A man of ordinary abilities will accomplish more with zeal and resolve than a man ten times more gifted without zeal and resolve. . . . Men who are possessed by these qualities commonly carry the day in almost all affairs. Most of the great things that have been done in the world, the great revolutions that have been accomplished in the kingdoms and empires of the earth, have been primarily owing to zeal and resolve. The very appearance of an intensely engaged personality, together with a fearless courage and unyielding resolve, in any person that has undertaken leadership in any human affair goes a long way toward accomplishing the intended outcome. . . . When people see a high degree of zeal and resolve in a person, it awes them and

has a commanding influence upon them. . . . But while we are cold and heartless and only go on in a dull manner, in an old formal round, we will never accomplish anything great. Our efforts, when they display such coldness and irresolution, will not even make people think of yielding. . . . The appearance of such indifference and cowardice does, as it were, provoke opposition.[6]

LOVE

The third treasure a church needs is love. "Let all that you do be done in love" (1 Cor. 16:14). With that one sentence, the apostle Paul brings all the gospel doctrine he has taught in 1 Corinthians to a practical conclusion. The beauty of love is the crown of a well-taught church.

How could it be otherwise? Christ himself is altogether lovely. In his sermon with that title, John Flavel helps us see our Lord's unmatched and unmixed beauty:

Christ infinitely transcends the most excellent and loveliest of created beings. Whatever loveliness is found in them, it is not without a distasteful tang. The fairest pictures must have their shadows. The rarest and most brilliant gems must have dark backgrounds to set off their beauty. The best creature is but a bittersweet at best. If there is something pleasing, there is also something distasteful. If a person has every excellence, both by nature and by grace, to delight us, yet there is also some natural corruption intermixed with it to put us off. But it is not so in our altogether lovely Christ. His excellencies are pure and unmixed. He is a sea of sweetness, without one drop of gall.[7]

This is who Christ is. He will always be to us an endless sea of sweetness. We will never taste one drop of gall in him. There is nothing in Christ we need to worry about. He is altogether sweet and lovely.

The implications for us in our human relationships are arresting. Christ, who is "near to the Father's heart" (John 1:18, NLT), has come into our world of brutality. He is present in his church today, and it shows. He brings tenderness, reasonableness, restraint, sincerity, and selfless care into our relationships with one another. We fail him in many ways. But we belong to the One who is altogether lovely, which means there can be nothing tawdry, cheap, sneaky, or nasty about us that should not be corrected immediately by his gospel. How will people on earth see the true beauty of our Head if his body below is scarred with ugliness, like everything else in this world? We have no right to disfigure his image upon us. Among the followers of Christ, beauty has authority.

Jesus told us that the unbelieving world will identify us as Christians only as we reflect his loveliness.[8] He said: "A new commandment I give to you, that you love one another: just as I have loved you, you also are to love one another. By this all people will know that you are my disciples, if you have love for one another" (John 13:34–35).

The command of Christ is that we love one another. The example of Christ is that we die for one another. The promise of Christ is that our love will show a skeptical world the difference he really makes. Love is Christ's authorized way for us to be convincing. People today don't care about doctrine, but they do care about love. The world is not impressed by anything about us but the love of Christ, nor should they be. *If we fail to love one another in ways so striking that we actually start looking like Jesus, then the world has the right to judge that we know nothing of him.* They might be wrong. We might indeed be Christians. But the world is right to dismiss unloving Christians as unchristian. Jesus himself gave them that right.

Jesus said even more. In John 17, he prayed not for the human race in general but for his people: "I am not praying for the world but for those whom you have given me . . . that they may all be one, just as you, Father, are in me, and I in you, that they also may be in us, so that the world may believe that you have sent me" (John 17:9, 21). Ultimate reality in the eternal Godhead is loving community, the Father at one with the Son, the Son at one with the Father. The world knows nothing of such intense, personal, unbroken unity. The world is divisive, angry, tense, and trigger-happy. The world does not believe that real unity can even exist. They have never seen it. All they have ever known is dog-eat-dog. But Jesus prayed for us, his church, that we would be a new kind of community here in this world. He prayed that our churches would be living proof of ultimate reality before the world today, so that more people might look beyond this world as they see in our churches—yes, our churches!—some reflection of the unity of the Father with the Son, and then believe the gospel.

As the magnitude of our Lord's prayer sinks in, can we think about all this without sorrow? How justifiably does the world look at divided churches and think: "When you Christians figure out how to get along, we might talk. But until then, we're not interested!" What's at stake among us Christians is nothing less than the testimony that the Father has sent the Son. It's not just our credibility at stake but Jesus's as the One sent from God.

The unity within our churches, as well as with all true Christians, born out of love, is not a little garnish on the side, if we happen to like that sort of thing. Our unity exalts Jesus in the eyes of the world as the true Son of God sent from the Father—all his claims convincing, all his purposes desirable, all his promises inevitable. This was important enough to Jesus that he *prayed* for it. Do we? Do we share his passion? Or do we treat it as an option while giving ourselves to our own priorities?

We bear living witness to Jesus as the Son of God by unity with all true Christians everywhere. This love for all true churches does not, I believe, require institutional sameness, but it certainly requires emotional identification. Our churches should rejoice over one another's successes and grieve over one another's setbacks. We should speak well of one another across denominational lines and humble ourselves in our own eyes by forgiving past injuries and promoting the common good in the gospel. Our loving Christ deserves a loving church in the world today!

Here are two illustrations of practical steps we can take toward real unity. The first comes from a pastor in my own city of Nashville who updated his church's website recently. One of the subpages is entitled "#sameteam."[9] The text reads:

> While we would love for you to be part of the CPC church family, we know it takes all kinds of churches to reach all kinds of people. God's kingdom is much larger than any single denomination or church! If for whatever reason you decide that CPC is not the church for you, there are many other good churches we could recommend. Here are some to consider . . .

Then the page offers a series of links to the websites of other churches in town—Presbyterian, Baptist, Anglican, and independent, all one in the gospel. This web page is a clear answer to our Lord's prayer that we would be one. And it is inconceivable that this selfless generosity of heart will go ignored. Love is always compelling. This pastor is bearing witness to the authority of the Son of God by his public solidarity with other true Christians.

A second illustration concerns reconciliation. Since we have not always loved one another with the beauty that turns heads, we should face our failures honestly. And we should heal our broken relationships as much as we can (Rom. 12:18). Sadly, "A brother offended is more unyielding than a strong city, and quarreling is like the bars of a castle" (Prov. 18:19). Oh, "the invisible walls of estrangement, so easy to erect, so hard to demolish"![10] Cruel words and deeds linger in the memory for decades, filtering down even to the next generation. Time erases nothing.

But Christ can redeem everything. When an offense breaks the loving unity of the body of Christ, we must follow his clear instructions: "Pay attention to yourselves! If your brother sins, rebuke him, and if he repents, forgive him, and if he sins against you seven times in the day, and turns to you seven times, saying, 'I repent,' you must forgive him" (Luke 17:3–4). There is deep wisdom in those simple words. They deserve careful meditation. Our Lord is very clear here, which we need. When we have wronged another or have been wronged ourselves, we tend to offer complicated evaluations of the difficulty. We tie ourselves up in knots with rules and procedures and, beneath those, our fear and pride. But all the procedural correctness on earth will fail to restore love if our hearts are bitter. Gratefully, our Lord's simple wisdom shines through if our hearts are soft. He shows us how to start moving toward one another, perhaps cautiously at first, but with healing power, when our hearts are broken.

I have been helped by the East Africa Revival and its emphasis on "walking in the light." Bishop Festo Kivengere, for example, tells how the Lord dealt with him:

> At one time William Nagenda and I were sharing an exhausting preaching itinerary overseas. Along the way I became jealous of the success of my brother. I became critical of everything he said. Each sentence was wrong or ungrammatical or unscriptural. His gestures were hypocritical. Everything about my brother was wrong, wrong, wrong. The more I criticized, the colder I became. I was icy and lonely and homesick. I was under conviction by the Holy Spirit, but I went on seeking to justify myself and put the blame on William. At last I repented and then had to face the difficult task of admitting my bad attitude to William. We were about to start off for a meeting where we were to preach together, and I said, "William, I am sorry. I'm very sorry. You sensed the coldness." "Yes, I felt the coldness, but I didn't know what had happened. What is it?" "I became jealous of you. Please forgive me." That dear brother got up and hugged me and we both shed tears of reconciliation. My heart was warm, and when he preached, the message spoke to me deeply.[11]

The verse that continually renewed the love of the African Christians was 1 John 1:7: "But if we walk in the light, as he is in the light, we have fellowship with one another, and the blood of Jesus his Son cleanses us from all sin." A heart aloof from God grows aloof from others. It engages in merciless comparisons and endless faultfinding. Therefore, all restoration begins by going back to God first, prodigals that we are.

The wonderful thing is that, when we lose our way, God is not hard to find again. He has made himself very findable. He is "in the light"—right out there in the place of truth, honesty, openness, confession, and owning up. God himself awaits us there. We sinners can go to him freely through the cross of Christ. There in the light, but only in the light, everything gets better in our relationships with one another too.

The price we pay is to face ourselves. That is humiliating and painful. It's why we shun the light. There are episodes in our past that we don't want to think about—harsh words, acts of betrayal, broken promises, and worse. We shove these memories down into the darkness of our excuses and blame-shifting. We refuse to call sin "sin." We feel too threatened by what we have done even to admit it to ourselves, much less confess it to others. But those places of deepest shame are where the Lord Jesus loves us the most tenderly. Is there any reason not to walk in his light together, where we recover fellowship with one another and the blood of Jesus cleanses us from all sin?

It is so refreshing to come back out into the light of honesty again, where we first met the Lord. It is there that ex-friends can be regained by love. It is there that Jesus is glorified in the eyes of the world.

Gospel doctrine creates a gospel culture.

SPECIAL THANKS

Thanks to the leaders and members of Immanuel Church Nashville, as we grow together in the gospel, both its doctrine and its culture.

Thanks to Mark Dever, Jonathan Leeman, and everyone at 9Marks. The trust you extended by inviting me to write this volume weighs on me with feelings of both my deep inadequacy and my high privilege.

Thanks to Crossway Books for your partnership in the gospel. You put the Lord first, above business, though you also conduct business with excellence.

Thanks to voices from the past who still speak—Martin Luther, John Calvin, Charles Haddon Spurgeon, Martyn Lloyd-Jones, Francis Schaeffer, Festo Kivengere, and especially my dad.

Thanks to my wife, Jani, for bearing the burden with me cheerfully and prayerfully. My dearest, you alone know.

NOTES

Introduction

1 William Tyndale, "A Pathway into the Holy Scripture," in *Doctrinal Treatises* (Cambridge: The University Press, 1848), 8. Style updated.

2 F. Blass and A. Debrunner, *A Greek Grammar of the New Testament and Other Early Christian Literature*, trans. Robert W. Funk (Chicago: The University of Chicago Press, 1973), § 119(1).

3 Whittaker Chambers, *Witness* (New York: Random House, 1952), 14. Edited for clarity.

4 D. Martyn Lloyd-Jones, *What Is an Evangelical?* (Edinburgh: Banner of Truth, 1992), 9–10. Lloyd-Jones continues: "The position of most of the Protestant churches today is almost the exact opposite of their position when they originally came into being. . . . It is no use assuming that because a thing has started correctly it is going to continue to be correct. There is a process at work, because of sin and evil, which tends to produce not only change but even degeneration."

5 Francis A. Schaeffer, "How Heresy Should Be Met," *Reformation Review*, July 1954, 9. Emphasis original.

6 A. W. Tozer, *Keys to the Deeper Life* (Grand Rapids: Zondervan, 1965), 8.

7 Raymond C. Ortlund, "Revival," Lake Avenue Congregational Church, February 1, 1976.

Chapter 1: The Gospel for You

1 Francis A. Schaeffer, *The Church Before the Watching World* (Downers Grove, IL: InterVarsity Press, 1971), 62.

2 Francis A. Schaeffer, *The Church at the End of the Twentieth Century* (Downers Grove, IL: InterVarsity Press, 1970), 107.

3 "Q & A: Anne Rice on Following Christ without Christianity," christianitytoday.com, posted August 17, 2010.

4 Greg Gilbert, *What Is the Gospel?* (Wheaton, IL: Crossway, 2010), 37–38.

5 John Piper, *Desiring God: Meditations of a Christian Hedonist* (Portland, OR: Multnomah Press, 1986), 78.

6 A. W. Tozer, *The Knowledge of the Holy* (New York: Harper & Row, 1961), 9.

7 Marcus Dods, *The Book of Genesis* (New York: A. C. Armstrong and Son, 1902), 161.

8 Reynolds Price, *Letter to a Man in the Fire* (New York: Scribner, 1999), 54.

9 W. H. Auden, *Selected Poems* (New York: Vintage, 2007), 96.

10 Lauren Slater, "The Trouble with Self-Esteem," *The New York Times*, February 3, 2002, www.nytimes.com/2002/02/03/magazine/the-trouble-with-self-esteem.html.

11 C. S. Lewis, *Mere Christianity* (New York: Macmillan, 1958), 40–41.

12 A. B. Bruce, *The Humiliation of Christ* (Edinburgh: T. & T. Clark, 1905), 334.

13 Octavius Winslow, *Personal Declension and Revival of Religion in the Soul* (London: Banner of Truth, 1962), 183–84. Emphasis original. Style updated.

14 Gerhard O. Forde, *Justification by Faith: A Matter of Death and Life* (Philadelphia: Fortress Press, 1982), 22.

15 Jonathan Edwards, *Works* (Edinburgh: Banner of Truth, 1979), I:687. Style updated.

Chapter 2: The Gospel for the Church

1 A faithful definition of a church, with more detail, is provided in Jonathan Leeman, *Church Membership: How the World Knows Who Represents Jesus* (Wheaton, IL: Crossway, 2012), 52.

2 Emily Esfahani Smith, "Relationships Are More Important Than Ambition," *The Atlantic*, April 16, 2013, www.theatlantic.com/health/archive/2013/04/relationships-are-more-important-than-ambition/275025/.

3 C. S. Lewis, "Membership," in *The Weight of Glory* (New York: HarperCollins, 2001), 174–75.

4 John Flavel, *The Whole Works of the Rev. Mr. John Flavel* (London: W. Baynes and Son, 1820), I:61. Style updated.

5 The ESV reads, ". . . having cleansed her." But the syntax of the Greek could also mean ". . . cleansing her" (NIV). The latter is more likely, in my opinion.

6 David Peterson, *Possessed by God: A New Testament Theology of Sanctification and Holiness* (Grand Rapids: Eerdmans, 1995), 52–53.

7 John Owen, *The Works of John Owen* (Edinburgh: Banner of Truth, 1980), II:63. Emphasis added.

8 See Francis A. Schaeffer, *The Finished Work of Christ* (Wheaton, IL: Crossway, 1998), 173–77.

Chapter 3: The Gospel for Everything

1 Harvie Conn, "Views of the City," *Third Way*, September 1989, 24.

2 Lesslie Newbigin, *The Open Secret: An Introduction to the Theology of Mission* (Grand Rapids: Eerdmans, 1995), 30–31.

3 Bob Dylan, "Everything Is Broken," *Oh Mercy* (Columbia Records, 1989).

4 John Calvin, *The Epistle of Paul the Apostle to the Hebrews* (Grand Rapids: Eerdmans, 1980), 9.

5 Jürgen Moltmann, *The Way of Jesus Christ: Christology in Messianic Dimensions* (Minneapolis: Fortress Press, 1993), 98–99. *Pars pro toto* is Latin for "a part representing the whole."

6 Dorothy Sayers, quoted in D. A. Carson, *The Gagging of God: Christianity Confronts Pluralism* (Grand Rapids: Zondervan, 1996), 53.

7 J. R. R. Tolkien, *The Return of the King* (Boston: Houghton Mifflin, 1994), 901.

8 Festo Kivengere, *Revolutionary Love* (Fort Washington, PA: Christian Literature Crusade, 1983), 60.

9 Jonathan Edwards, *Charity and Its Fruits* (London: Banner of Truth, 1969), 327–28. Style updated.

10 Augustine, cited in Peter Brown, *Augustine of Hippo* (Berkeley: University of California Press, 1967), 297–98.

11 Martin Luther, cited in Theodore G. Tappert, ed., *Luther: Letters of Spiritual Counsel* (Philadelphia: Westminster Press, 1955), 86–87.

Chapter 4: Something New

1 Francis Schaeffer, *2 Contents, 2 Realities* (Downers Grove, IL: InterVarsity Press, 1975), 25, also 1–32.

2 Christian Smith, *Soul Searching: The Religious and Spiritual Lives of American Teenagers* (Oxford: Oxford University Press, 2005), 162–71.

3 Ibid., 163.

4 Elton Trueblood, *The Incendiary Fellowship* (New York: Harper & Row, 1967), 107–8.

5 Francis A. Schaeffer, *Speaking the Historic Christian Position into the 20th Century* (privately published, 1965), 125–26.

6 John Calvin, *Institutes of the Christian Religion*, ed. John T. Mc-Neill, trans. Ford Lewis Battles, Library of Christian Classics, vols. 20–21 (Louisville: Westminster John Knox, 1960), 4.1.21.

7 A full and helpful discussion is available in Jonathan Leeman, *Church Discipline: How the Church Protects the Name of Jesus* (Wheaton, IL: Crossway, 2012).

8 Edmund P. Clowney, *The Church* (Downers Grove, IL: InterVarsity Press, 1995), 30.

9 Peter Collier and David Horowitz, *Destructive Generation: Second Thoughts about the Sixties* (New York: Summit Books, 1989), 80.

10 From the hymn "I Love Thy Kingdom, Lord" by Timothy Dwight, 1800.

11 I thank John Piper for suggesting this line of thought in private correspondence.

Chapter 5: It Isn't Easy, But It Is Possible

1 Martin Luther, *A Commentary on St. Paul's Epistle to the Galatians* (London: James Clarke & Co., 1953), 40. Style updated.

2 I thank my son Dr. Eric Ortlund for helping me articulate this.

3 John Bunyan, *Grace Abounding* (Cambridge: The University Press, 1907), 71–72. Emphasis original. Style updated.

4 ESV: "rubbish." But a stronger translation, along the lines of

the KJV's "dung," is warranted. See Moisés Silva, *Philippians* (Grand Rapids: Baker Book House, 1992), 180.

5 Charles Haddon Spurgeon, "The Church—Conservative and Aggressive," *The Metropolitan Tabernacle Pulpit*, Vol. XII (Pasadena, TX: Pilgrim Publications, 1977), 366. Preached May 19, 1861. Emphasis original.

6 A. W. Tozer, "True Faith Brings Committal," in *The Root of the Righteous* (Harrisburg: Christian Publications, 1955), 50.

7 John R. W. Stott, *The Message of Galatians* (London: Inter-Varsity Press, 1968), 49.

8 *Mishnah*, Oholoth, 18.7.

9 Paul Tournier, *Guilt and Grace* (New York: Harper & Row, 1962), 15–16.

10 Martin Luther, *Galatians* (Wheaton, IL: Crossway, 1998), 111–12. Edited slightly.

Chapter 6: What We Can Expect

1 R. V. G. Tasker, *The Second Epistle of Paul to the Corinthians* (Grand Rapids: Eerdmans, 1974), 57.

2 Bruce K. Waltke, *Genesis: A Commentary* (Grand Rapids: Zondervan, 2001), 142. Emphasis added.

3 John Calvin, *The Second Epistle of Paul the Apostle to the Corinthians* (Grand Rapids: Eerdmans, 1980), 35.

4 D. Martyn Lloyd-Jones, *Revival* (Westchester, IL: Crossway Books, 1987), 300.

5 Charles Haddon Spurgeon, "The Two Effects of the Gospel," *The New Park Street Pulpit*, Vol. I (Pasadena, TX: Pilgrim Publications, 1981), 198. Preached May 27, 1855.

6 John Piper, cited in Justin Taylor, "Tozer's Contradiction and His Approach to Piety," Between Two Worlds blog, June 8, 2008, thegospelcoalition.org/blogs/justintaylor/2008/06/08/tozers-contradiction-and-his-approach_08/.

Chapter 7: Our Path Forward

1 Eric J. Alexander, "A Plea for Revival," in *Our Great God and Savior* (Edinburgh: Banner of Truth, 2010), 174. Emphasis added.

2 James Denney, quoted in James S. Stewart, *Heralds of God* (New York: Charles Scribner's Sons, 1946), 74.

3 Henry Drummond, quoted in Raymond C. Ortlund, *Let the Church Be the Church* (Waco: Word, 1983), 44.

4 John Heuss, *Our Christian Vocation* (Greenwich: The Seabury Press, 1955), 15–16.

5 Howard W. Guinness, *Sacrifice* (Chicago: InterVarsity Press, 1947), 59–60.

6 Jonathan Edwards, "Thoughts on the Revival," in *Works* (Edinburgh: Banner of Truth, 1979), I:424. Style updated.

7 John Flavel, "He Is Altogether Lovely," in *The Whole Works of the Reverend Mr. John Flavel* (London: Thomas Parkhurst, 1701), I:332. Style updated.

8 This argument, from John 13 and 17, echoes Francis A. Schaeffer, *The Mark of the Christian* (Downers Grove, IL: InterVarsity Press, 1970), 7–16.

9 christpres.org/sameteam.

10 Derek Kidner, *The Proverbs: An Introduction and Commentary* (Downers Grove, IL: InterVarsity Press, 1964), 130.

11 Festo Kivengere, quoted in Richard K. MacMaster and Donald R. Jacobs, *A Gentle Wind of God: The Influence of the East Africa Revival* (Scottsdale: Herald Press, 2006), 212.

GENERAL INDEX

SCRIPTURE INDEX

9Marks

Building Healthy Churches

9Marks exists to equip church leaders with a biblical vision and practical resources for displaying God's glory to the nations through healthy churches.

To that end, we want to see churches characterized by these nine marks of health:

1   Expositional Preaching
2   Biblical Theology
3   A Biblical Understanding of the Gospel
4   A Biblical Understanding of Conversion
5   A Biblical Understanding of Evangelism
6   Biblical Church Membership
7   Biblical Church Discipline
8   Biblical Discipleship
9   Biblical Church Leadership

Find all our Crossway titles
and other resources at
www.9Marks.org

9MARKS: BUILDING HEALTHY CHURCHES SERIES

This series from 9Marks features a short, readable book on each of the nine marks originally introduced by Pastor Mark Dever's best-selling book, *Nine Marks of a Healthy Church* (plus one additional book on doctrine).

Useful for group or individual study, these concise books will help you grasp what the Bible says about the local church and how to build a healthy congregation.

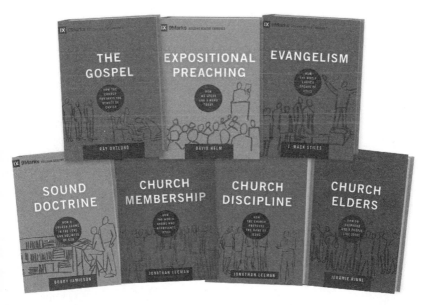

 For more information, visit crossway.org.